CONTENTS

- 2 Key to Map Pages
- 3 Key to Map Symbols
- 4-23 Road Maps at 9 miles to 1 inch
- 24-25 Dublin Route Planning Map
- 26-33 City / Town Plans and Information

  - 26-27 Dublin
  - 28-29 Belfast
  - 30-31 Cork
  - 32-33 Limerick

- 34-36 Tourist Information Centres
- 37-54 Places of Interest
- 55-64 Index to place names

Collins Handy Road Atlas Ireland

Collins
An Imprint of HarperCollins*Publishers*
77–85 Fulham Palace Road, Hammersmith, London W6 8JB

© HarperCollins*Publishers* 1996

All rights reserved. No part of this publication may be reproduced, in a retrieval system, or transmitted, in any form or by any means, electronic, mechanical, photocopying, recording or otherwise without the prior written permission of the publisher and copyright owner.

The contents of this edition of the Collins Handy Road Atlas Ireland are believed to be correct at the time of printing. Nevertheless, the publishers can accept no responsibility for errors or omissions, changes in the detail given or for any expense or loss thereby caused.

Printed by The Edinburgh Press Ltd in Scotland

ISBN 0 00 448259 X   CDNE   HB 8111

KEY TO MAP PAGES

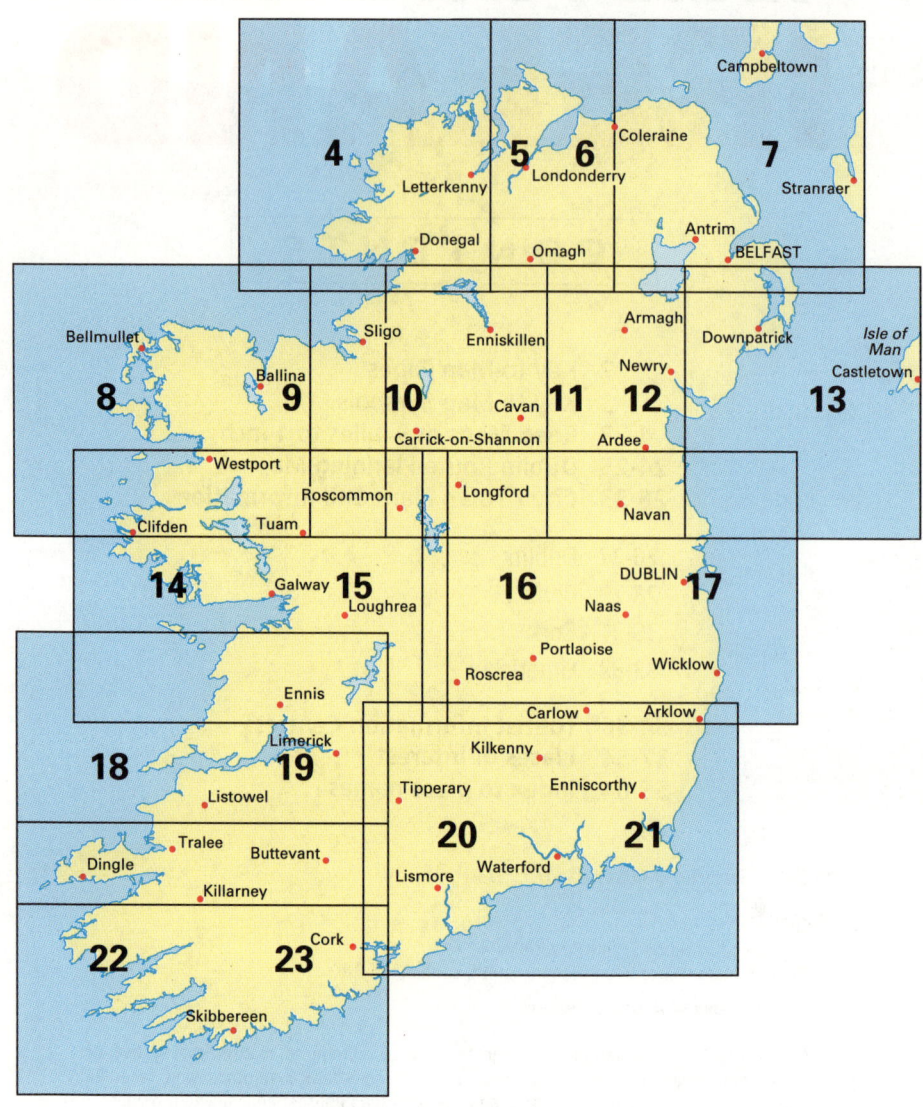

KEY TO SYMBOLS

Roads	Features	Additional information on city & town plans pages 26-33
Motorway (under constr.)	Airport	Main road / throughroute
Junction number (restricted access)	National boundary	Pedestrian street
Primary / national route (dual carriageway)	County boundary	Shopping street
'A' road (dual carriageway, under constr.)	National park	Place of interest
'B'/ regional road (dual carriageway, under constr.)	Forest park	Railway station
Other road	Urban area	Car park
Road distances (in miles)	Beach	Public toilets
Gradient	Canal	Police station
Border crossing point	Height in metres	Cathedral / Church
Railway	Place of interest	One way street
Car ferry	Tourist information (all year / seasonal)	

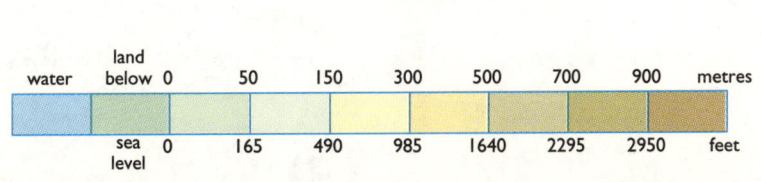

Scale: approx. 9 miles to 1 inch
0 — 10 — 20 miles
0 — 10 — 20 — 30 km

water	land below sea level	0	50	150	300	500	700	900	metres
		0	165	490	985	1640	2295	2950	feet

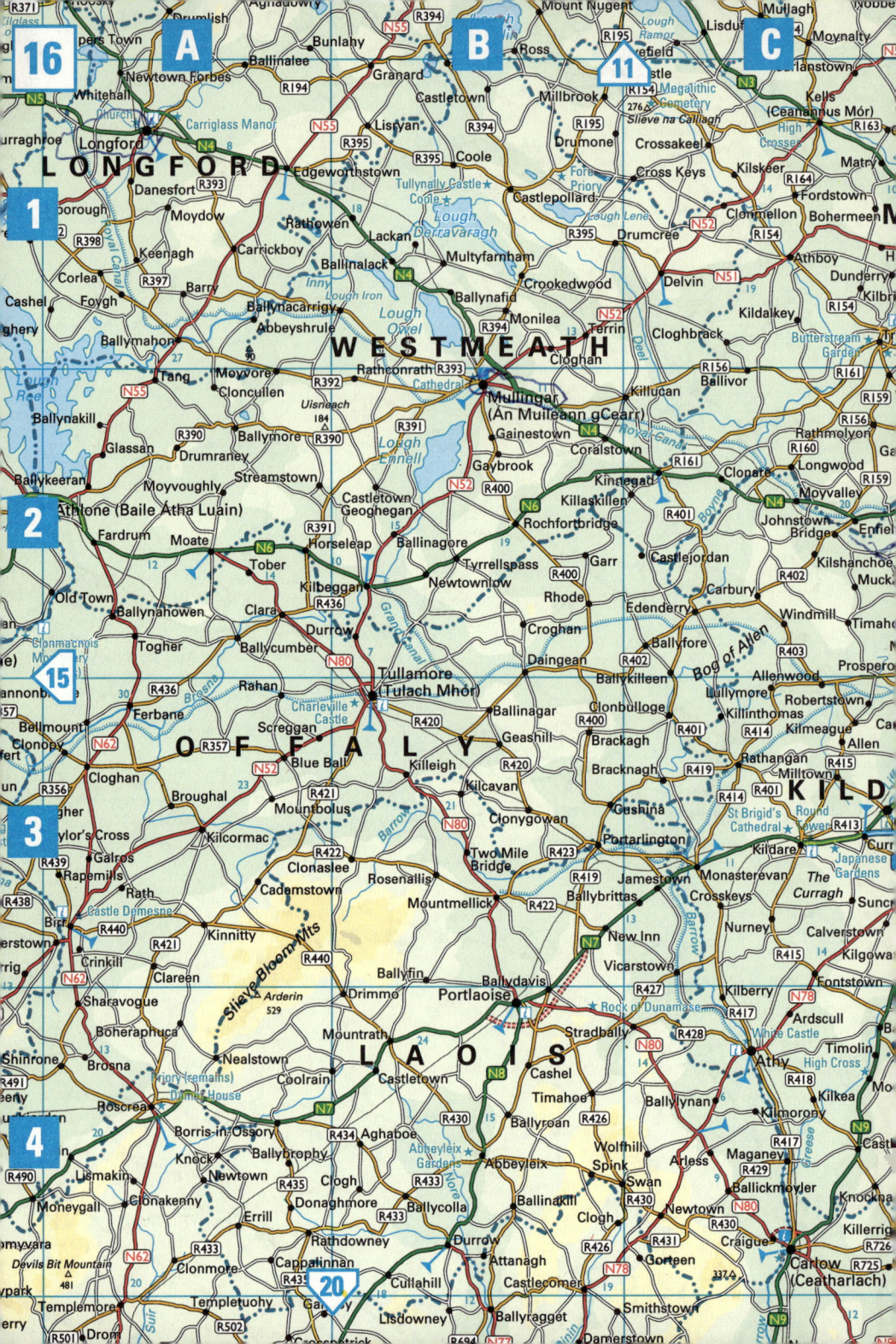

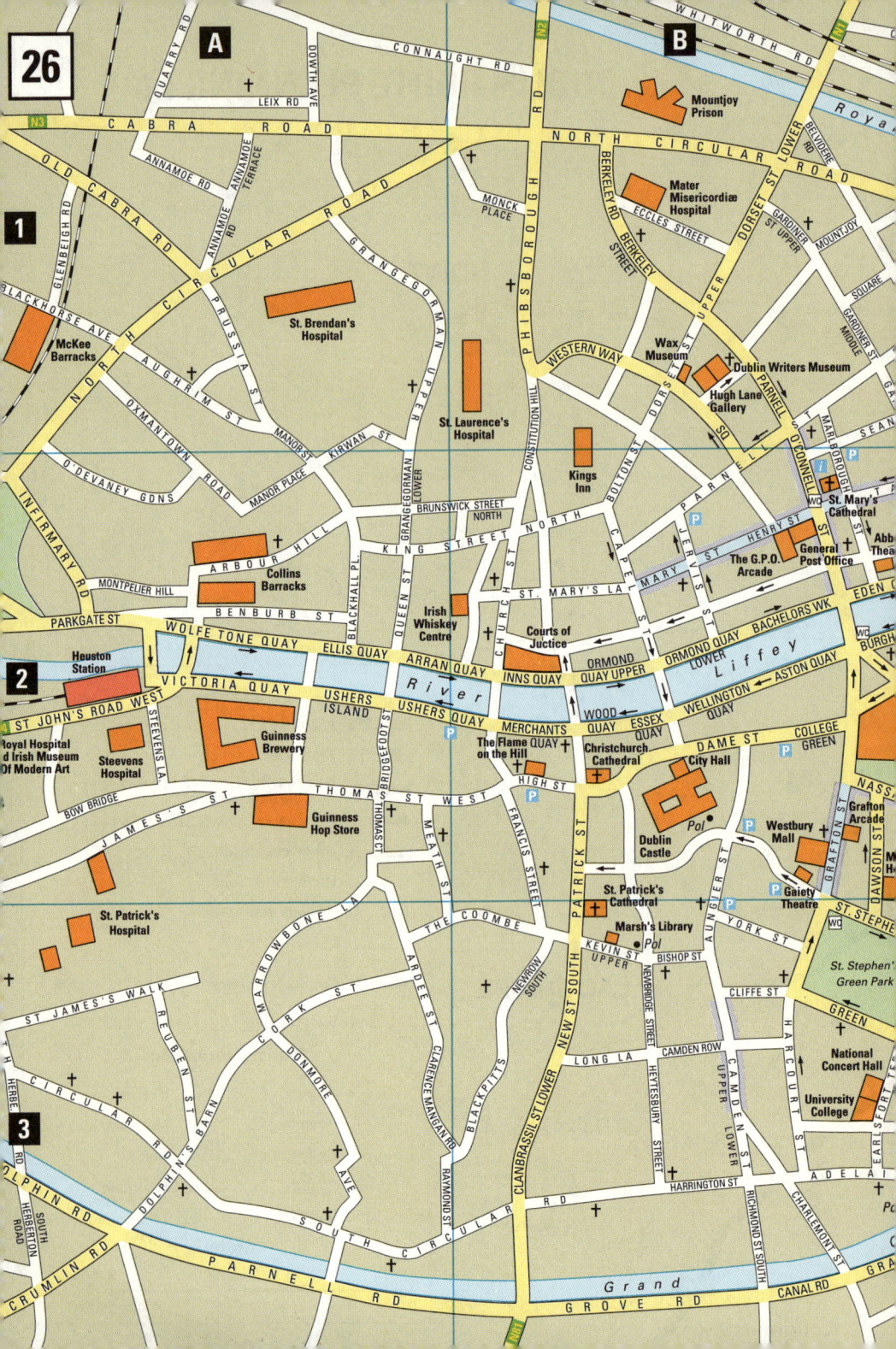

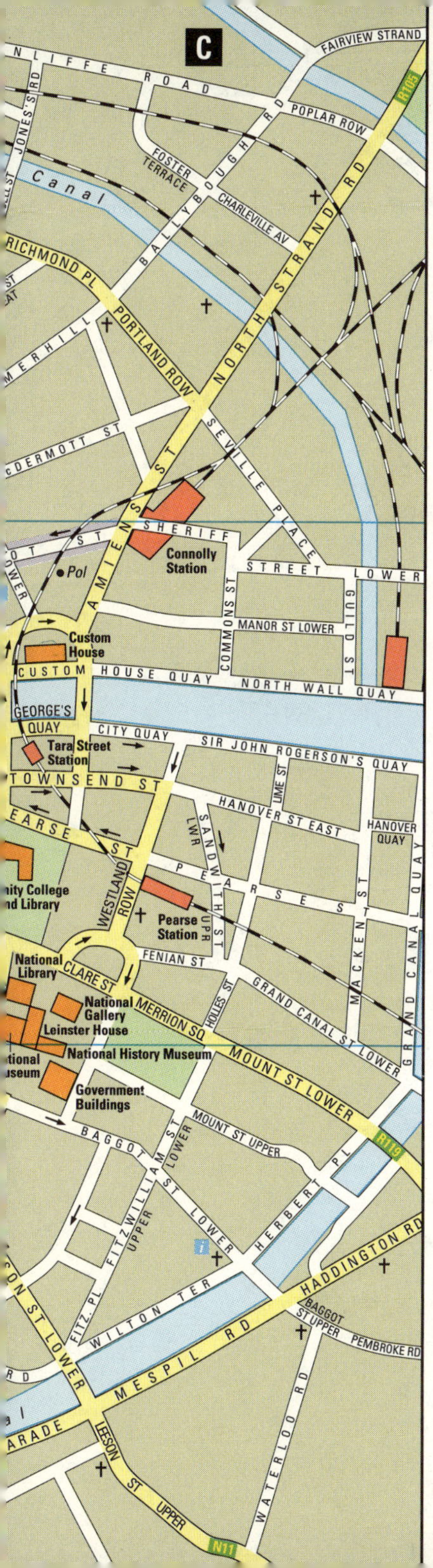

DUBLIN

27

INDEX TO STREET NAMES

Street	Grid	Street	Grid	Street	Grid
Adelaide Rd	B3	Essex Quay	B2	Nassau St	B2
Amiens St	C2	Fairview Strand	C1	New St S	B3
Annamoe Rd	A1	Fenian St	C2	Newbridge St	B3
Annamor Ter	A1	Fitzwilliam Pl	C3	Newrow S	B3
Arbour Hill	A2	Fitzwilliam St Lower	C3	North Circular Rd	A1
Ardee St	A3	Fitzwilliam St Upper	C3	North Strand Rd	C1
Arran Quay	A2	Foster Ter	C1	North Wall Quay	C2
Aston Quay	B2	Francis St	B2	O'Connell St	B1
Aughrim St	A1	Gardiner St Lower	B1	O'Devaney Gdns	A2
Aungier St	B3	Gardiner St Middle	B1	Old Cabra Rd	A1
Bachelors Wk	B2	Gardiner St Upper	B1	Ormond Quay Lower	B2
Baggot St Lower	C3	George's Quay	C2	Ormond Quay Upper	B2
Baggot St Upper	C3	Glenbeigh Rd	A1	Oxmantown Rd	A1
Ballybough Rd	C1	Grafton St	B2	Parkgate St	A2
Belvidere Rd	B1	Grand Canal Quay	C2	Parnell Rd	A3
Benburb St	A2	Grand Canal St Lower	C2	Parnell Sq	B1
Berkeley Rd	B1	Grand Parade	B3	Parnell St	B2
Berkeley St	B1	Grangegorman Lower	A2	Patrick St	B3
Bishop St	B3	Grangegorman Upper	A1	Pearse St	C2
Blackhall Pl	A2	Grove Rd	B3	Pembroke Rd	C3
Blackhorse Av	A1	Guild St	C2	Phibsborough Rd	B1
Blackpitts	B3	Haddington Rd	C3	Poplar Row	C1
Bolton St	B2	Hanover Quay	C2	Portland Row	C1
Bow Bridge	A2	Hanover St E	C2	Prussia St	A1
Bridgefoot St	A2	Harcourt St	B3	Quarry Rd	A1
Brunswick St N	A2	Harrington St	B3	Queen St	A2
Burgh Quay	B2	Henry St	B2	Raymond St	A3
Cabra Rd	A1	Herbert Pl	C3	Reuben St	A3
Camden Row	B3	Herberton Rd	A3	Richmond Pl	C1
Camden St Lower	B3	Heytesbury St	B3	Richmond St S	B3
Camden St Upper	B3	High St	B2	Russell St	C1
Canal Rd	B3	Holles St	C2	Sandwith St Lower	C2
Capel St	B2	Infirmary Rd	A2	Sandwith St Upper	C2
Charlemont St	B3	Inns Quay	B2	Sean McDermott St	B1
Charles St Great	B1	James's St	A2	Seville Pl	C1
Charleville Av	C1	Jervis St	B2	Sheriff St Lower	C2
Church St	B2	Jones's Rd	C1	Sir John Rogerson's Quay	C2
City Quay	C2	Kevin St Upper	B3	South Circular Rd	A3
Clanbrassil St Lower	B3	Kildare St	C3	South Herberton Rd	A3
Clare St	C2	King St N	A2	St. James's Wk	A3
Clarence Mangan Rd	A3	Kirwan St	A2	St. John's Rd W	A2
Cliffe St	B3	Leeson St Lower	C3	St. Mary's La	B2
Clonliffe Rd	B1	Leeson St Upper	C3	St. Stephen's Grn	B3
College Grn	B2	Leix Rd	A1	Steevens La	A2
Commons St	C2	Lime St	C2	Summerhill	B1
Connaught Rd	A1	Long La	B3	Talbot St	B2
Constitution Hill	B2	Macken St	C2	The Coombe	A3
Cork St	A3	Manor Pl	A2	Thomas Ct	A2
Crumlin Rd	A3	Manor St	A1	Thomas St W	A2
Custom House Quay	C2	Manor St Lower	C2	Townsend St	C2
Dame St	B2	Marlborough St	B1	Ushers Island	A2
Dawson St	B2	Marrowbone La	A3	Ushers Quay	A2
Dolphin Rd	A3	Mary St	B2	Victoria Quay	A2
Dolphin's Barn	A3	Meath St	A2	Waterloo Rd	C3
Donmore Av	A3	Merchants Quay	B2	Wellington Quay	B2
Dorset St Lower	B1	Merrion Sq	C2	Western Way	B1
Dorset St Upper	B1	Mespil Rd	C3	Westland Row	C2
Dowth Av	A1	Monck Pl	B1	Whitworth Rd	B1
Earlsfort Ter	B3	Montpelier Hill	A2	Wilton Ter	C3
Eccles St	B1	Mount St Lower	C3	Wolfe Tone Quay	A2
Eden Quay	B2	Mount St Upper	C3	Wood Quay	B2
Ellis Quay	A2	Mountjoy Sq	B1	York Rd	B3

INDEX TO PLACES OF INTEREST

Place	Grid	Place	Grid	Place	Grid
Abbey Theatre	B2	Kings Inn	B2	St. Laurence's Hospital	B1
Christchurch Cathedral	B2	Leinster House	C2	St. Mary's Cathedral	B2
City Hall	B2	Mansion House	B2	St. Patrick's Cathedral	B3
Collins Barracks	A2	Marsh's Library	B3	St. Patrick's Hospital	A3
Connolly Station	C2	Mater Misericordiae Hospital	B1	St. Stephen's Green Park	B3
Courts of Justice	B2	McKee Baracks	A1	Steevens Hospital	A2
Custom House	C2	Mountjoy Prison	B1	Tara St Station	C2
Dublin Castle	B2	National Concert Hall	B3	The Flame on the Hill	B2
Dublin Writers Museum	B1	National Gallery	C2	The G.P.O. Arcade	B2
Gaiety Theatre	B2	National History Museum	C3	Trinity College and Library	C2
General Post Office	B2	National Library	C2	University College	B3
Grafton Arcade	B2	National Museum	C2	Wax Museum	B1
Guinness Brewery	A2	Pearse Station	C2	Westbury Mall	B2
Guinness Hop Store	A2	Royal Hospital and Irish Museum of Modern Art	A2		
Heuston Station	A2				
Hugh Lane Gallery	B1	St. Brendan's Hospital	A1		
Irish Whiskey Centre	B2				

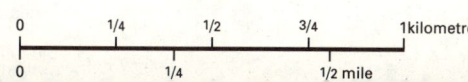

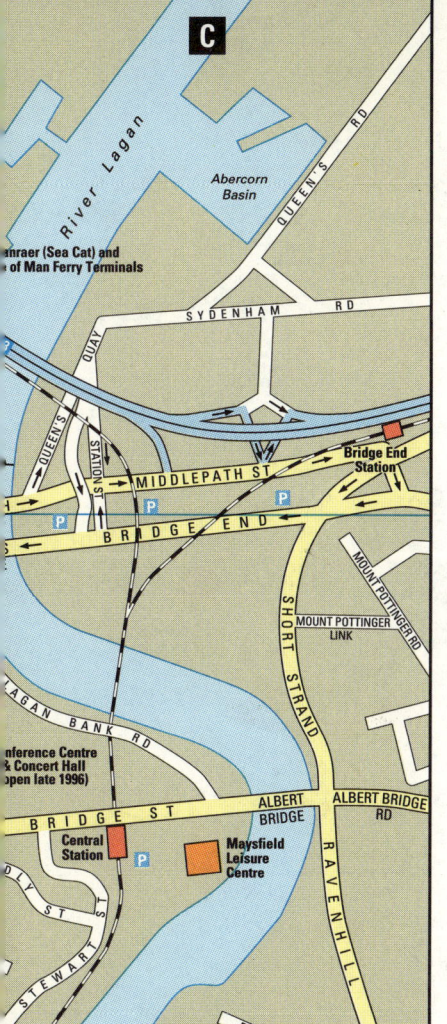

BELFAST

INDEX TO STREET NAMES

Academy St	B1	Donegall Sq N	B2	North Queen St	B1
Adelaide St	B2	Donegall Sq S	B2	North St	B1
Agnes St	A1	Donegall Sq W	B2	Northumberland St	A1
Albert Bridge	C2	Donegall St	B1	Oak Way	B3
Albert Bridge Rd	C2	Dover St	A1	Ormeau Av	B2
Albert Sq	B1	Dublin Rd	B3	Ormeau Embankment	C3
Albert St	A2	Dunbar Link	B1	Ormeau Rd	B3
Alfred St	B2	Dunbar St	B1	Oxford St	B2
Amelia St	B2	Dunluce Av	A3	Percy Pl	A1
Ann St	B2	Durham St	A2	Percy St	A1
Antrim Rd	A1	East Bridge St	B2	Peter's Hill	A1
Balfour Av	C3	Elmwood Av	A3	Posnett St	B3
Ballarat St	C2	Essex St	B3	Queen Elizabeth Bridge	B1
Bankmore St	B2	Eureka Dr	A3	Queen St	B2
Bedford St	B2	Exchange St	B1	Queen's Bridge	C1
Bendigo St	C3	Falls Rd	A2	Queen's Quay	C1
Bentham Dr	A3	Fitzroy Av	B3	Queen's Rd	C1
Berry St	B2	Fitzwilliam St	A3	Queen's Sq	B1
Beverley St	A1	Francis St	B1	Raphael St	B2
Blythe St	A3	Franklin St	B2	Ravenhill Rd	C2
Botanic Av	B3	Frederick St	B1	Regent St	A1
Boundary St	A1	Friendly St	B2	River Ter	B3
Bradbury Pl	B3	Glengall St	A2	Roden St	A2
Bridge End	C2	Great Georges St	B1	Rosemary St	B1
Bridge St	B1	Great Patrick St	B1	Ross Rd	A2
Brown Sq	A1	Great Victoria St	B2	Rowland Way	B2
Brown St	A1	Gresham St	B1	Royal Av	B1
Bruce St	B2	Grosvenor Rd	A2	Rugby Av	B3
Brunswick St	B2	Hamilton St	B2	Rugby Rd	B3
Cameron St	B3	High St	B2	Salisbury St	B3
Carlow St	A1	Hope St	A2	Sandy Row	A2
Carmel St	B3	Hopewell Av	A1	Scott St	A3
Carrick Hill	B1	Hopewell Cres	A1	Servia St	A2
Castle Pl	B2	Howard St	B2	Shaftesbury Sq	B3
Castle St	B2	Huss Row	A1	Shankill Par	A1
Charlotte St	B3	John St	A2	Shankill Rd	A1
Chichester St	B2	Joy St	B2	Short Strand	C2
Clarence St	B2	Lagan Bank Rd	C2	Smithfield Sq N	B1
Clifton St	B1	Library St	B1	Stanley St	A2
College Grn	B3	Lindsay St	B3	Station St	C1
College Pk	B3	Linenhall St	B2	Stewart St	C2
College Sq	B2	Linfield St	A2	Sydenham Rd	C1
College Sq N	A2	Lisburn Rd	A3	Talbot St	B1
Cooke St	B3	Little Donegall St	B1	Tomb St	B1
Coolmore St	A3	Little Patrick St	B1	Townsend St	A1
Cornmarket	B2	Lower Cres	B3	Ulsterville Av	A3
Corporation Sq	B1	Lower Stanfield St	B2	Union St	B1
Corporation St	B1	Malone Rd	A3	University Av	B3
Crimea St	A1	Malone Rd	A3	University Sq	B3
Cromac St	B2	Maryville St	B3	University St	B3
Cromwell Rd	B3	May St	B2	Upper Queen St	B2
Crumlin Rd	A1	McAuley St	B2	Ventry St	B3
Cullingtree Rd	A2	McClure St	B3	Vernon St	B3
Denmark St	A1	Middlepath St	C1	Victoria Sq	B2
Distillery St	A2	Millfield	A1	Victoria St	B2
Divis St	A2	Montgomery St	B2	Walnut St	B3
Donegall Pass	B3	Mount Pottinger Link	C2	Waring St	B1
Donegall Pl	B2	Mount Pottinger Rd	C2	Wellington Pl	B2
Donegall Quay	B1	Nelson St	B1	Wellwood St	A3
Donegall Rd	A3	North Howard Link	A1	Westlink	A3
Donegall Sq E	B2	North Howard St	A2	York St	B1

INDEX TO PLACES OF INTEREST

Arts Council Gallery	B2	Crafts Gallery	B2	Royal Belfast Academical	
Arts Theatre	B3	Custom House	B1	Institution	A2
B.B.C.	B2	General Post Office	B2	Royal Courts of Justice	B2
Botanic Station	B3	Great Northern Mall	B2	Smithfield Market	B1
Bridge End Station	C1	Great Victoria St Station	A2	Spires Mall	B2
Castlecourt Centre	B1	Grosvenor Hall	A2	St. Anne's Cathedral	B1
Central Station	C2	Group Theatre	B2	St. Peter's Cathedral	A2
Cinema	B3	Hipark Centre	B2	Stranraer (Sea Cat) and	
City Hall	B2	Lagan Weir	B1	Isle of Man Ferry	
City Hospital	A3	Linenhall Library	B2	Terminals	C1
City Hospital Station	A3	Maysfield Leisure Centre	C2	Ulster Hall	B2
Clock Tower	B1	Millfield Technical College	A1	University of Ulster	B1
College of Further		Opera House	B2	Victoria Centre	B2
Education	C3	Ormeau Leisure Centre	C3		
Conference Centre		Ormeau Park	C3		
and Concert Hall		Queen's University	B3		
(open late 1996)	C2	Ross's Court	B2		

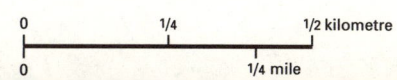

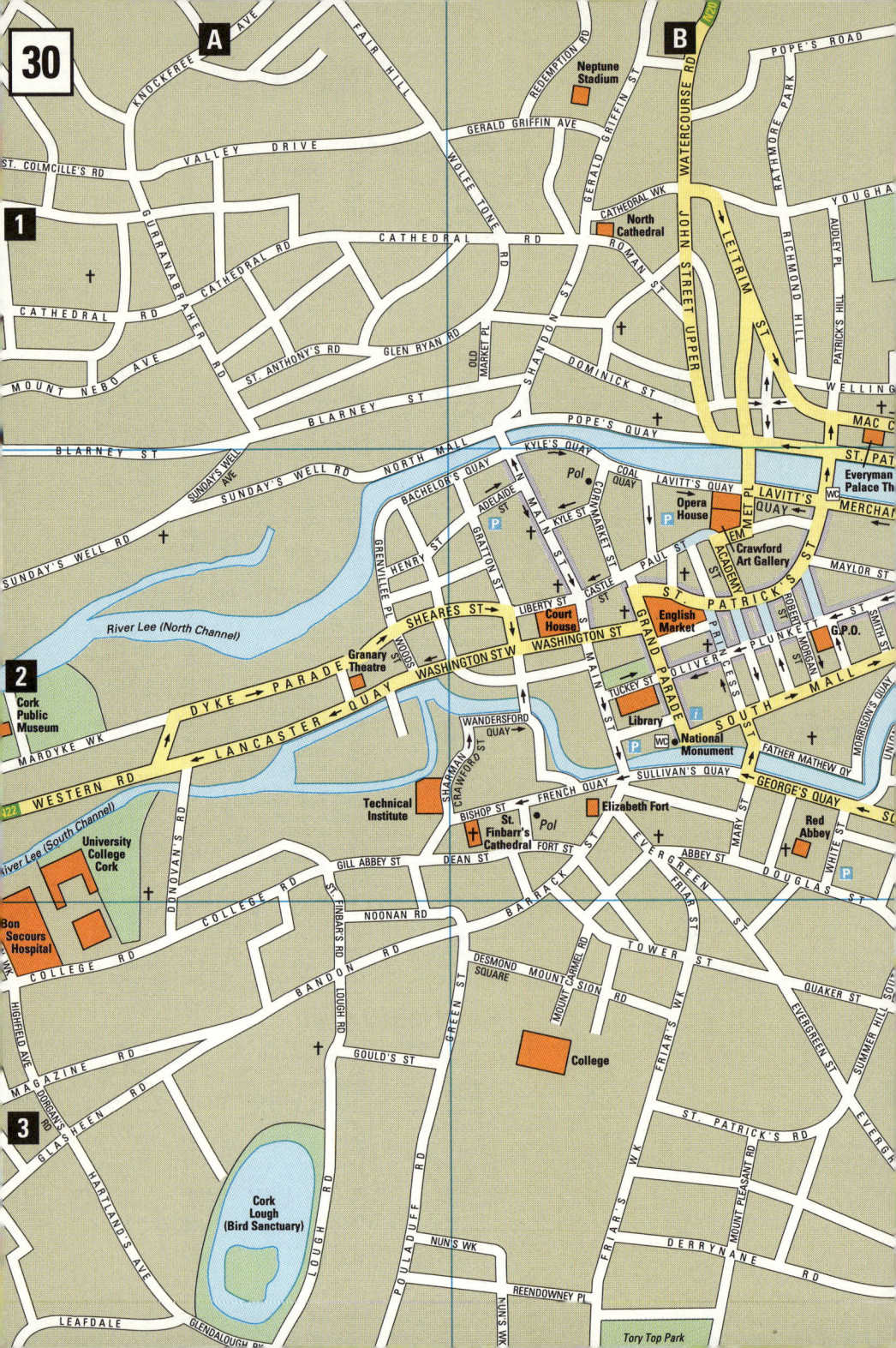

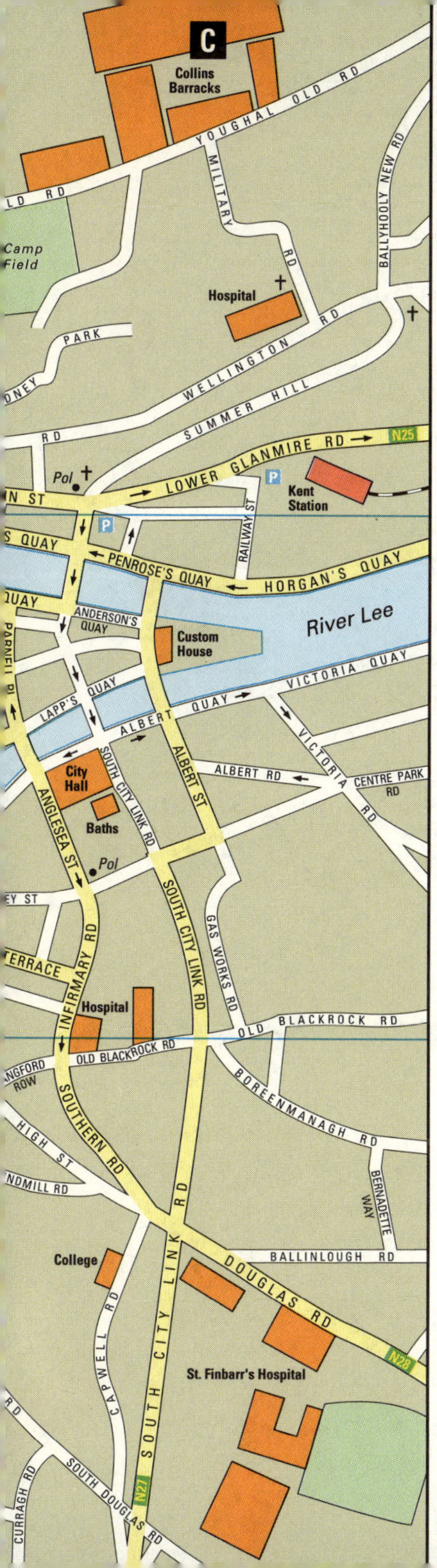

CORK

INDEX TO STREET NAMES

Street	Grid	Street	Grid	Street	Grid
Abbey St	B2	Glen Ryan Rd	A1	Pope's Quay	B1
Academy St	B2	Glendalough Pk	A3	Pope's Rd	B1
Adelaide St	B2	Glenville Rd	A2	Pouladuff Rd	A3
Albert Quay	C2	Gould's St	A3	Princess St	B2
Albert Rd	C2	Grand Par	B2	Quaker St	B3
Albert St	C2	Gratton St	B2	Railway St	C2
Anderson's Quay	C2	Green St	B3	Rathmore Pk	B1
Anglesea St	C2	Gurranabraher Rd	A1	Reendowney Pl	B3
Audley Pl	B1	Hartland's Av	A3	Richmond Hill	B1
Bachelor's Quay	A2	Henry St	A2	Robert St	B2
Ballinlough Rd	C3	High St	C3	Roman St	B1
Ballyhooly New Rd	C1	Highfield Av	A3	Shandon St	B1
Bandon Rd	A3	Horgan's Quay	C2	Sharman Crawford St	A2
Barrack St	B3	Infirmary Rd	C2	Sheares St	A2
Bernadette Way	C3	John Street Upper	B1	Sidney Pk	C1
Bishop St	B2	Knockfree Av	A1	Smith St	B2
Blarney St	A1	Kyle St	B2	South City Link Rd	C2
Boreenmanagh Rd	C3	Kyle's Quay	B1	South Douglas Rd	C3
Capwell Rd	C3	Lancaster Quay	A2	South Main St	B2
Castle St	B2	Langford Row	C3	South Mall	B2
Cathedral Rd	A1	Lapp's Quay	C2	South Terr	B2
Cathedral Wk	B1	Lavitt's Quay	B2	Southern Rd	C3
Centre Park Rd	C2	Leafdale	A3	St. Anthony's Rd	A1
Coal Quay	B2	Leitrim St	B1	St. Colmcille's Rd	A1
College Rd	A3	Liberty St	B2	St. Finbarr's Rd	A2
Copley St	B2	Lough Rd	A3	St. Patrick's Quay	B2
Cornmarket St	B2	Lower Glanmire Rd	C1	St. Patrick's Rd	B3
Curragh Rd	C3	Mac Curtain St	B1	St. Patrick's St	B2
Dean St	A2	Magazine Rd	A3	Sullivan's Quay	B2
Derrynane Rd	B3	Mardyke Wk	A2	Summer Hill	C1
Desmond Sq	B3	Mary St	B2	Summer Hill S	B3
Dominick St	B1	Maylor St	B2	Sunday's Well Av	A2
Donovan's Rd	A2	Merchant's Quay	B2	Sunday's Well Rd	A2
Dorgan's Rd	A3	Military Rd	C1	Tower St	B3
Douglas Rd	C3	Morgan St	B2	Tuckey St	B2
Douglas St	B2	Morrison's Quay	B2	Union Quay	B2
Dyke Par	A2	Mount Carmel Rd	B3	Valley Dr	A1
Emmet Pl	B2	Mount Nebo Av	A1	Victoria Quay	C2
Evergreen Rd	B3	Mount Pleasant Rd	B3	Victoria Rd	C2
Evergreen St	B2	Mount Sion Rd	B3	Wandersford Quay	B2
Fair Hill	A1	Noonan Rd	A3	Washington St	B2
Father Mathew Quay	B2	North Main St	B2	Washington St W	B2
Fort St	B2	North Mall	A2	Watercourse Rd	B1
French Quay	B2	Nun's Wk	A3	Wellington Rd	B1
Friar St	B2	O'Connell Av	B3	Western Rd	A2
Friar's Wk	B3	Old Blackrock Rd	C3	White St	B2
Gaol Wk	A3	Old Market Pl	B1	Windmill Rd	C3
Gas Works Rd	C2	Oliver Plunkett St	B2	Wolfe Tone Rd	B2
George's Quay	B2	Parnell Pl	C2	Woods St	A2
Gerald Griffin St	B1	Patrick's Hill	B1	Youghal Old Rd	B1
Gill Abbey St	A2	Paul St	B2		
Glasheen Rd	A3	Penrose's Quay	C2		

INDEX TO PLACES OF INTEREST

Place	Grid	Place	Grid	Place	Grid
Baths	C2	Elizabeth Fort	B2	Red Abbey	B2
Bon Secours Hospital	A3	English Market	B2	St. Finbarr's Cathedral	B2
Camp Field	C1	Everyman Palace Theatre	B1	St. Finbarr's Hospital	C3
City Hall	C2			Technical Institute	A2
Collins Barracks	C1	General Post Office	B2	Tory Top Park	B3
Cork Lough (Bird Sanctuary)	A3	Granary Theatre	A2	University College, Cork	A2
		Kent Station	C1		
Cork Public Museum	A2	National Monument	B2		
Court House	B2	Neptune Stadium	B1		
Crawford Art Gallery	B2	North Cathedral	B1		
Custom House	C2	Opera House	B2		

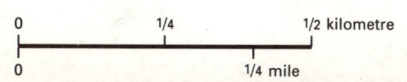

LIMERICK

INDEX TO STREET NAMES

Street	Grid	Street	Grid	Street	Grid
Aherne's Row	C1	Grattan St	C2	Parnell St	B3
Anne St	B2	Hartstone St	A3	Patrick St	B2
Arthur's Quay	B2	Harvey's Quay	A2	Perry Sq	B3
Athlunkard St	C1	Henry St	A3	Perry St	B3
Baals Bridge	C1	High Rd	B1	Post Office La	B3
Bank Pl	B1	High St	C2	Quinlan St	A3
Barrack La	C2	Honan's Quay	B2	Robert St	B2
Barrington St	A3	Howley's Quay	A2	Roches Row	B3
Bedford Row	B2	Hyde Rd	B3	Roches St	B2
Belfield Gdns	A1	Island Row	C1	Roxborough Av	C3
Bishop St	B1	James St	C2	Roxborough Rd	C3
Boherbuoy	B3	John's Sq	C2	Rutland St	B2
Brennan's Row	C2	John's St	C2	Sarsfield Bridge	A2
Bridge St	B1	Lady's La	B3	Sarsfield St	B2
Broad St	C2	Liddy St	B2	Sean Heuson Pl	C2
Carr St	C2	Little Catherine St	B2	Sexton St	B3
Castle St	B1	Little Gerald Griffin St	C2	Shannon St	A2
Cathedral Pl	C3	Little William St	B2	Sir Harry's Hall	C1
Catherine Pl	B3	Lock Quay	C1	St. Alphonsus St	A3
Catherine St	B3	Long La	C1	St. Augustine Pl	B1
Cecil St	B3	Lower Cecil St	A2	St. Frances St	B1
Chapel St	B2	Lower Gerald Griffin St	C2	St. Lelia St	C2
Charlotte Quay	C1	Lower Glentworth St	A3	St. Peter St	B1
Clancy's Strand	B1	Lower Hartstone St	A3	Steam Boat Quay	A3
Clare St	C1	Lower Mallow St	A3	Summer La	C2
Condell Rd	A2	Mallow St	B3	The Bishops Quay	A2
Convent St	B1	Mary St	C1	The Crescent	A3
Cornmarket Row	C2	Mathew Bridge	B1	The Parade	B1
Crosbie Row	B1	Merchant's Quay	B1	The Shannon Bridge	A2
Cruises St	B2	Michael St	B2	Theatre La	A3
Curry La	C2	Mill La	A3	Thomas St	B2
Davis St	B3	Mt Kennedy Pl	A3	Thomond Bridge	B1
Denmark St	B2	Mulgrave St	C3	Thomond Row	A1
Dock Rd	A3	Mungret St	C2	Todd's Row	B2
Dominic St	B3	New Rd	C2	Upper Denmark St	B2
Ellen St	B2	Newenham St	A3	Upper Gerald Griffin St	B3
Ennis Rd	A1	Newgate La	B1	Upper Henry St	B3
Exchange St	B1	Nicholas St	B1	Upper Mallow St	B3
Farranshone Rd	A1	O'Callaghan's Strand	A2	Upper William St	C2
Frances St	B2	O'Connell St	A3	Vereker Gdns	A1
Gaol La	C1	O'Curry St	A3	Wickham St	B3
Gary Owen Rd	C2	O'Dwyer Bridge	C1	William La	C2
Georges Quay	B1	Old Clare St	C2	William St	B2
Glentworth St	B3	Old Windmill Rd	C2	Windmill St	A3

INDEX TO PLACES OF INTEREST

Place	Grid	Place	Grid	Place	Grid
Art Gallery	B3	Daniel O'Connell Monument	A3	St. John's Hospital	C2
Arthur's Quay Centre	B2			St. Mary's Cathedral	B1
Arthur's Quay Park	B2	General Post Office	B2	St. Mary's Town House	C1
Belltable Arts Centre	A3	King John's Castle	B1	Theatre Royal	B3
Bishop's Palace	B1	Limerick City Archives & Library	B2	Treaty Stone	B1
Bus & Railway Station	B3				
City Wall	C2	Limerick Museum	C2		
Civic Centre & City Hall	B1	Peoples Park	B3		
Court House	B1	Priory Park	B3		
Curragower Park	B1	Regional Maternity Hospital	A1		
Custom House	B1				
Custom House Park	B1	St. John's Cathedral	C2		

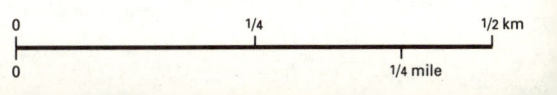

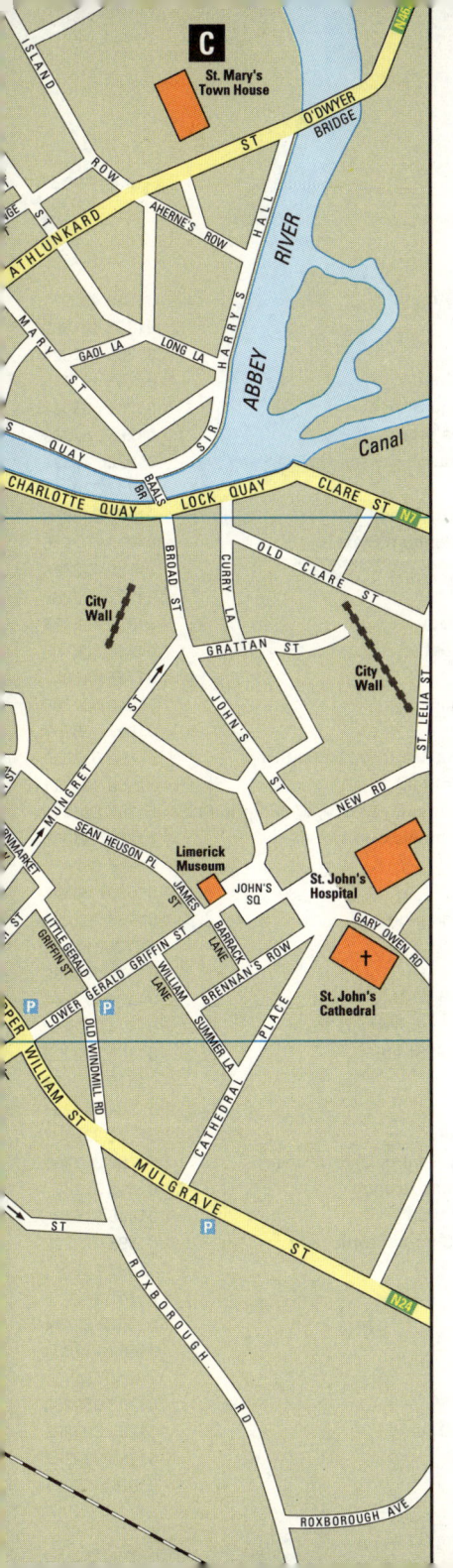

TOURIST INFORMATION CENTRES

KEY
* ✱ Summer opening only
* ⌕ Room reservation services

Northern Ireland
Area Codes are for the UK and Northern Ireland

✱ Antrim, Co. Antrim	⌕ Pogue's Entry, Church Street	☏ 01849 428331
Armagh, Co. Armagh	⌕ 40 English Street	☏ 01861 521800
Ballycastle, Co. Antrim	⌕ 7 Mary Street	☏ 012657 62024
Ballymena, Co. Antrim	Ardeevin, 80 Galgorm Road	☏ 01266 44111
✱ Ballymena, Co. Antrim	Morrows Shop, 17 Bridge Street	☏ 01266 653663
Ballymoney, Co. Antrim	⌕ Raida House, 14 Charles Street	☏ 012656 62280
Banbridge, Co. Down	⌕ Gateway Tourist Information Centre, Newry Road	☏ 018206 23322
Bangor, Co. Down	⌕ 34 Quay Street	☏ 01247 270069
Belfast, Co. Antrim	⌕ St. Annes Court, 59 North Street	☏ 01232 246609
Belfast, Co. Antrim	⌕ Belfast City Airport, Sydenham Bypass	☏ 01232 457745
Belfast, Co Antrim	⌕ International Airport	☏ 01849 422888
Belfast, Co. Down	53 Castle Street	☏ 01232 327888
Carnlough, Co. Antrim	⌕ Post Office, Harbour Road	☏ 01574 885238
Carrickfergus, Co. Antrim	⌕ Knight Ride, Antrim Street	☏ 01960 366455
Coleraine, Co. Londonderry	⌕ Railway Road	☏ 01265 44723
Cookstown, Co. Tyrone	Council Office, Burn Road	☏ 016487 62205
✱ Cookstown, Co. Tyrone	⌕ 48 Molesworth Street	☏ 016487 66727
Downpatrick, Co. Down	⌕ Downpatrick/Ardglass Railway, 74 Market Street	☏ 01396 612233
Dungannon, Co. Tyrone	⌕ Council Offices, Circular Road	☏ 01868 725311
Enniskillen, Co. Fermanagh	⌕ Fermanagh Tourist Information Centre, Wellington Rd	☏ 01365 323110
Giant's Causeway, Co. Antrim	⌕ 44 Causeway Road, Bushmills	☏ 012657 31855
Hillsborough, Co. Down	The Square	☏ 01846 682477
Kilkeel, Co. Down	⌕ 6 Newcastle Street	☏ 016937 62525
Killymaddy, Co. Tyrone	⌕ Ballygawley Road, Dungannon	☏ 01868 767259 & 725311
Larne, Co. Antrim	⌕ Narrow Gauge Road	☏ 01574 260088
✱ Larne, Co. Antrim	Carnfunnock County Road, Coast Road	☏ 01574 270541
✱ Larne, Co. Antrim	Sir Thomas Dixon Buildings, Victoria Road	☏ 01574 272313
Limavady, Co. Londonderry	⌕ Council Offices, 7 Connell Street	☏ 015047 22226
Lisburn, Co. Antrim	⌕ Market Square	☏ 01846 660038
Londonderry, Co. Londonderry	⌕ 8 Bishop Street	☏ 01504 267284
Lurgan, Co. Armagh	Town Hall, 6 Union Street	☏ 01762 323757
Lurgan, Co. Armagh	Lough Neagh Discovery Centre, Oxford Island	☏ 01762 322205
Magherafelt, Co. Londonderry	⌕ Council Offices, 43 Queens Avenue	☏ 01648 32151
✱ Magherafelt, Co. Londonderry	⌕ The Bridewell, Church Street	☏ 01648 31510
Newcastle, Co. Down	⌕ The Newcastle Centre, Central Promenade	☏ 013967 22222
Newry, Co. Down	⌕ Town Hall	☏ 01693 68877
Newtownards, Co. Down	2 Church Street	☏ 01247 812215
Newtownstewart, Co. Tyrone	⌕ 21 - 27 Moyle Court	☏ 016626 62414
Omagh, Co. Tyrone	⌕ 1 Market Street	☏ 01662 247831 & 240774
Portadown, Co. Armagh	Town Hall	☏ 01762 353260
✱ Portrush, Co. Antrim	⌕ Dunluce Centre, Sandhill Drive	☏ 01265 823333
✱ Portstewart, Co. Londonderry	⌕ Town Hall, The Crescent	☏ 01265 832286
Sion Mills, Co. Tyrone	⌕ Melmount Road	☏ 016626 58027

✻ Sperrin Herigate Centre, Co. Tyrone	274 Glenelly Road, Cranagh	☎ 016626 48142
Strabane, Co. Tyrone	Council Offices, 47 Derry Road	☎ 01504 382204
✻ Strabane, Co. Tyrone	Abercorn Square	☎ 01504 883735
Warrenpoint, Co. Down	Town Hall, Church Street	☎ 016937 52256

Republic of Ireland
Area Codes are for Republic of Ireland

✻ Achill, Co. Mayo	Achill Island	☎ 098 45384
✻ Adare, Co. Limerick	Heritage Centre	☎ 061 396255
✻ Aran Islands (Kilronan), Co. Galway	Inishmore, Aran Islands	☎ 099 61263
Ardmore, Co. Galway	Main Street, Ardmore	☎ 024 94444
Arklow, Co. Wicklow	Town Hall	☎ 0402 32484
✻ Athlone, Co. Westmeath	Athlone Castle	☎ 0902 94630
Athy, Co. Kildare	Town Hall, Emily Square	☎ 0507 31859
✻ Aughrim		☎ 0905 73939
✻ Ballina, Co. Mayo	Cathedral Road	☎ 096 70848
✻ Ballinasloe, Co. Galway	Kellers Travel	☎ 0905 42131
✻ Bantry, Co. Cork	The Square	☎ 027 50229
✻ Birr, Co. Offaly	Rosse Row	☎ 0509 20110
Blarney, Co. Cork		☎ 021 381624
✻ Boyle, Co. Roscommon	King House	☎ 079 62145
✻ Buncrana, Co. Donegal	Shore Front	☎ 077 62600
✻ Bundoran, Co. Donegal	Main Street	☎ 072 41350
✻ Caherciveen, Co. Kerry	RIC Barracks	☎ 066 72589
✻ Cahir, Co. Tipperary	Castle Car Park	☎ 052 41453
Carlow, Co. Carlow	Cathedral Close, Tullow Street	☎ 0503 31554
✻ Carrick-on-Shannon, Co. Leitrim	The Marina	☎ 078 20170
✻ Cashel, Co. Tipperary	Town Hall	☎ 062 61333
✻ Castlebar, Co. Mayo	The Lineen Hall Centre, Lineen Hall Street	☎ 094 21207
✻ Cavan, Co. Cavan	Farnham Street	☎ 049 31942
✻ Clifden, Co. Galway	Market Street	☎ 095 21163
✻ Cliffs of Moher (Liscannor), Co. Clare		☎ 023 33226
✻ Clonmacnois, Co. Offaly		☎ 0905 74134
Clonmel, Co. Tipperary	Nelson Street, Clonmel	☎ 052 22960
Cork City, Co Cork	Tourist House, Grand Parade	☎ 021 273251
Cork Airport, Co. Cork	Airport Terminal	☎ Freephone
✻ Dingle, Co. Kerry	Main Street	☎ 066 51188
✻ Donegal Town, Co. Donegal	The Quay	☎ 073 21148
✻ Drogheda, Co. Louth		☎ 041 37070
Dublin City, Co. Dublin, Tourist Information		☎ 01 284 4768
Dublin Credit Card Reservations		☎ 01 284 1765
Dublin City, Co. Dublin	14 Upper O'Connell Street	
Dublin City, Co. Dublin	Baggot Street Bridge	
Dublin City, Co. Dublin	Arrivals Hall, Dublin Airport	
Dublin City, Co. Dublin	B & I Terminal	
Dundalk, Co. Louth	Jocelyn Street	☎ 042 35484
Dungarvan, Co. Louth	Town Centre	☎ 058 41741
✻ Dungloe, Co. Donegal	Main Street	☎ 075 21297

Dún Laoghaire, Co. Dublin	Terminal Building, Dún Laoghaire Harbour	☎ 01 284 4768
Ennis, Co. Clare	Clare Road	☎ 065 28366
✳ Enniscorthy, Co. Wexford	Castle Museum	☎ 054 34699
Galway, Co. Galway	Victoria Place, Eyre Square	☎ 091 63081
✳ Glengarriff, Co. Cork	Main Street	☎ 027 63084
Gorey, Co. Wexford	Town Centre	☎ 055 21248
✳ Kenmare, Co. Kerry	Heritage Centre	☎ 064 41233
Kerry County Airport (Farranfore)	Terminal Building	☎ 066 64399
✳ Kildare Town, Co. Kildare	The Market House	☎ 045 522696
✳ Kilkee, Co. Clare		☎ 065 56112
Kilkenny, Co. Kilkenny	Shee Alms House, Rose Inn Street	☎ 056 51500
✳ Killaloe, Co. Kilkenny	Heritage Centre	☎ 061 376866
Killarney, Co. Kerry	Town Hall	☎ 064 31633
✳ Kilrush, Co. Clare	Town Hall	☎ 065 51577
✳ Kinsale, Co. Cork	Pier Road	☎ 021 772234
✳ Knock Airport, Co. Mayo	The Shrine, Terminal Building	☎ 094 67247
✳ Knock Village, Co. Mayo		☎ 094 88193
✳ Laragh, Co. Wicklow	Glendalough Tourist Information Office, Glendalough	☎ 0404 45482
Letterkenny, Co. Donegal	Derry Road	☎ 074 21160
Limerick City, Co. Limerick	Arthur's Quay	☎ 061 317522
✳ Listowel, Co. Kerry	St. John's Church	☎ 068 22590
✳ Longford, Co. Longford	Main Street	☎ 043 46566
✳ Louisburgh, Co. Mayo	Bridge Street	☎ 098 66400
✳ Midleton, Co. Cork	Jameson Heritage Centre	☎ 021 613702
✳ Monaghan, Co. Monaghan	Market House	☎ 047 81122
Mullingar, Co. Westmeath	Dublin Road	☎ 044 48650
✳ Nenagh, Co. Tipperary	Connolly Street	☎ 067 31610
Newbridge, Co. Kildare		☎ 045 33835
✳ Newgrange, Co. Meath	Newgrange, Slane	☎ 041 24274
✳ New Ross, Co. Wexford	Kennedy Centre	☎ 051 21857
Oughterard, Co. Galway	Main Street	☎ 091 82808
✳ Portlaoise, Co. Laois	James Fintan Lawlor Avenue	☎ 0502 21178
✳ Roscommon, Co. Roscommon	Harrison Hall	☎ 0903 26342
✳ Rosslare Harbour (Kilrane), Co. Wexford		☎ 053 33232
Rosslare Terminal, Co. Wexford	Rosslare Harbour	☎ 053 33622
✳ Salthill, Co. Galway		☎ 091 63081
Shannon Airport, Co. Clare	Terminal Building	☎ 061 471664
Skibbereen, Co. Cork	Town Hall	☎ 028 21766
Sligo, Co. Sligo	Áras Reddan, Temple Street	☎ 071 61201
✳ Thoor Ballylee, Co. Galway	Thoor Ballylee, Gort	☎ 091 31436
Tipperary Town, Co. Tipperary	James Street	☎ 062 51457
Tralee, Co. Kerry	Ashe Memorial Hall, Denny Street	☎ 066 21288
✳ Tramore, Co. Waterford	Railway Square	☎ 051 381572
✳ Trim, Co. Meath	Heritage Centre, Millstreet	☎ 046 37111
✳ Tuam, Co. Galway	The Mill Museum, Tuam	☎ 093 24463
✳ Tullamore, Co. Offaly		☎ 0506 52617
Waterford, Co. Waterford	41 The Quay	☎ 051 75788
Westport, Co. Mayo	The Mall	☎ 098 25711
✳ Wexford, Co. Wexford	Crescent Quay	☎ 053 23111
Wicklow, Co. Wicklow	Rialto Centre, Fitzwilliam Square	☎ 0404 69117
✳ Youghal, Co. Cork	Heritage Centre	☎ 024 92390

PLACES OF INTEREST

ADARE *County Limerick* 19 E2

The pretty village of Adare, which once belonged to the Kildare Fitzgeralds, and then the Earls of Dunraven, has several items of interest. The Gothic Revival manor house, now a luxury hotel, was built by the 2nd Earl in 1832 to his own design with additional work by James Pain and A.W. Pugin. The main hall is defined by stone arches and a handsome rococo staircase while the ornamental gardens are splendid for strolling. Medieval Desmond Castle, overlooking the River Maigue, still retains a fine square keep, as well as two great halls a kitchen and stables. The most splendid remains in Adare are those of the 15th century Franciscan Friary (located in the grounds of the Adare Manor Golf Club) which can be admired from the long medieval bridge on the N20 to the north of the village.

AILLWEE CAVE *County Clare* 15 D3

A short way south of Ballyvaughan, at the edge of the limestone plateau known as the Burren, Aillwee Cave, was discovered in 1940 by a local shepherd. Well over 2 million years old, the tunnel, some 0.75 of a mile in length, is filled with stalagmites and stalactites and an illuminated underground river and waterfall.

BALLINTOBER CASTLE (or TOBERBRIDE) *County Roscommon* 9 F4

Just outside the village of Ballintober of Bridget is this ruin of a huge castle dating back to about 1300. It was the principal seat of the O'Connor dynasty from the time of the Anglo-Norman invasions until the 18th century when they moved to Clonalis. Many times besieged, rarely breached, it is without a keep, but retains its twin-towered gatehouse and corner towers.

BELFAST CATHEDRAL *Belfast* 28 B1

Close to the intersection of Clifton, Donegall and York Streets and Royal Avenue, St Anne's is the Protestant Cathedral for the dioceses of Connor and Down-and-Dromore. Built in 1898, in Romanesque style, it includes mosaics by Gertrude Stein, has some very fine stained glass and is the burial place of Lord Carson, the leader of the opposition to Home Rule who died in 1935.

BELLEEK POTTERY *County Fermanagh*   10 B1

The pottery was established in the small village of Belleek in 1857 by John Caldwell Bloomfield who had inherited nearby Castle Caldwell. A keen amateur potter, he noticed that all the necessary ingredients - feldspar, water, kaolin and so on - were available locally. Within ten years, award winning highly decorated, lustrous parian ware was being made and a tour of the attractive works demonstrates its continuing production. A shop and a small museum are attached to the works.

BIRR CASTLE DEMESNE *County Offaly*   16 A3

Birr Castle has been occupied by the Parsons family since 1620 when Sir Laurence Parsons built most of the current building. Twice beseiged in the late 17th century, the Gothic facade was added in the 19th century. Although the castle is only occasionally opened to the public, the gardens are open daily and consist of a beautifully landscaped collection of trees and shrubs, the tallest box hedge in the world, and a kitchen garden, all set around a lake and waterfalls. An unusual feature is the case of the Great Telescope, built in the 1840s by the 3rd Earl of Rosse and the largest in the world until 1917. Exhibitions about the castle demesne are held in the stables.

BLARNEY CASTLE & BLARNEY STONE *County Cork*   23 F2

The castle is just southwest of the village of Blarney. The keep, standing on a rocky outcrop, amid 18th century parkland, was built in 1446 by Cormac MacCarthy and then lost by the MacCarthys in the 17th century, finally passing to the Colthursts who built the nearby 19th century house. The Blarney Stone lies just beneath the battlements. According to the rhyme 'A stone that whoever kisses, O he never misses to grow eloquent' but the origin of this bizarre piece of hokum is unknown, although it is said that Dermot MacCarthy was expert in using honeyed language to keep the English at bay in the 16th century.

BOYLE ABBEY *County Roscommon*   10 B3

The impressive remains of the 12th century Cistercian abbey known as Mainister na Buaille are on the north side of the market town of Boyle and are the burial place of Ireland's most famous medieval religious poet, Donnchadh Mor O'Daly, who may have been abbot here. Although badly damaged by Cromwell's army, the abbey is one of the best preserved in the country. The church is a fine example of the transition from Romanesque to Gothic and has particularly interesting carvings on the arcade capitals, whilst elsewhere the gatehouse, kitchen and cloister are all clearly in evidence.

BUNRATTY CASTLE *nr. Limerick, County Clare* 19 E2

The original design of the roof was unknown and during the restoration was a matter of conjecture, but the remaining, magnificent keep of Bunratty Castle has been restored to how it looked at the time of its construction on the banks of the Ratty in 1460. It was probably built by the MacNamaras but was soon in the hands of the O'Briens, who became the Earls of Thomond and who occupied the castle until 1712. Widely admired in its heyday, the three storeyed keep retains its corner towers and massive arches. Inside is the vaulted entrance hall, with so-called 'sheila-na-gig` (female fertility figure) in the wall, and chapel and cellars with 16th century stucco work. Many of the rooms are filled with a fine collection of period furniture, whilst mock banquets regularly evoke the castle's colourful past. The nearby folk park has examples of traditional Irish houses and agricultural machinery and demonstrations of ancient skills.

BUNRATTY CASTLE & FOLK PARK *County Clare* 19 E2

The magnificently restored castle is described above. At its base is the folk park, a collection of buildings and artefacts that illustrate Ireland's rural life at the turn of the century. Some of the buildings were moved here from an original site elsewhere whilst others are replicas. Traditional cottages from hill and valley areas of the Shannon region are represented, as well as a blacksmiths workshop, a mill, and an entire village as it would have been at the turn of the 19th century. Demonstrations of traditional skills are regularly given.

CAHIR CASTLE *Cahir, County Tipperary* 20 B2

A pretty town, Cahir boasts this impressive castle, the largest of its type in the country, which sits on a rocky outcrop in the middle of the River Suir at the foot of the Galty Mountains. It dates back to the 15th century and was inappropriately restored in 1840. However, behinds its walls are a huge keep, a furnished great hall and two courts. Notwithstanding its solid appearance it was frequently overrun and in 1650 surrendered to Cromwell without coming to battle. There is also an exhibition on Gaelic laws and customs.

CARRICK-A-REDE ROPEBRIDGE *County Antrim*   6 C2

This curiosity, north of Ballycastle, is a 66 ft bridge of planks with wire handrails swinging 80 ft above the sea and rocks separating Larrybane Cliffs from a small rocky island. There are magnificent views out to sea to be enjoyed during the intrepid journey across the bridge. This bridge has been erected here every spring for 200 years or more for the fishermen who operate a salmon fishery on the island.

CARRICKFERGUS CASTLE *Carrickfergus, County Antrim*   7 E4

Carrickfergus dates back to the end of the 12th century but is very well preserved. Among the historical events associated with it are the landing of William of Orange in 1690 and the first action by an American ship in European waters in 1778. There remain three medieval courtyards within the walls containing a massive keep, with barrel-vaulted chambers and Great Hall. It contains a goodly selection of armour and armaments.

CARROWEKEEL *County Sligo*   10 A2

About 4 miles northwest of Ballinafad, just west of Lough Arrow, on the Bricklieve Mountains, is the remote site of Carrowkeel Bronze-Age passage-tomb cemetery. The setting consists of the site of an ancient village and 14 chambered cairns. It is not sure if the village, consisting of some 70 circular huts, and the burial ground, are from the same era but the cemetery, which contained cremated remains and was clearly planned, is undoubtedly one of the most important in the country.

CASTLE COOLE *County Fermanagh*   10 C1

Recently restored by the National Trust, this elegant house, the seat of the Earls of Belmore, was designed in neo-Classical style by James Wyatt and Richard Johnston at the end of the 18th century. The facade is of Portland Stone whilst the interior plaster work, of classical simplicity, was undertaken by Joseph Rose in rooms still filled with their original furniture. The lake is the home of Ireland's only breeding colony of Greylag Geese.

CASTLECALDWELL *nr. Leggs, County Fermanagh*   **10 B1**
The Caldwell family was responsible for the local porcelain industry, and their ruined 17th century castle is situated in a wooded peninsula on the banks of Lower Lough Erne. There are inspiring views across the lough from the gardens where wildfowl hides permit visitors to gaze undisturbed at the flocks of waterfowl that breed here, including the largest breeding colony of black scoter duck in the British Isles.

CASTLETOWN HOUSE *Celbridge, County Kildare*   **17 D2**
Just outside the Liffeyside village of Celbridge, Castletown, built in 1722 for the Speaker of the Irish House of Commons, William Conolly, is perhaps the largest private house in Ireland. Consisting of a central block in early Georgian or Palladian style, flanked by colonnades, Castletown was designed by the Florentine, Alessandro Galilei, and Edward Pearce, architect of the Dublin Parliament. The house has been restored through the work of the Irish Georgian Society.

CASTLEWARD HOUSE *Strangford, County Down*   **13 D2**
Situated in 600 acres of parkland, Castleward House, now the property of the National Trust, is a half Gothic, half Palladian masterpiece built in 1765 for the 1st Viscount Bangor and his wife, each of whom favoured different styles. The family furniture is still in place, whilst the Trust has recreated a Victorian laundry. Close to the house is Old Castle Ward, a small Plantation castle built in 1610.

CHRIST CHURCH CATHEDRAL *Dublin*   **26 B2**
The cathedral church of the Protestant archdiocese of Dublin and Glendalough, and the principal religious and ceremonial church for the former English regime, is at the heart of the medieval city. It has been the scene for many notable events, including

the coronation of Lambert Simnel as Edward VI in 1487. The first cathedral was built here in 1038 and a replacement begun over a century later. Various additions were made over the following centuries but after the nave vaulting collapsed in 1562 it went through a period of neglect. Eventually the whole church was remodelled in Gothic Revival style by G.E. Street, who was also responsible for the covered footbridge linking the cathedral to the Synod Hall. The interior has some fine surviving medieval sections including the groin-vaulted crypt, and transepts, all of which date back to the 12th century, and a sprinkling of interesting monuments including the casket containing the heart of St Laurence, and the figure of Robert, 19th Earl of Kildare.

CLOGHAN (Clononey) CASTLE *County Offaly*   15 F3

A little way to the northwest of the village of Cloghan, Clononey Castle was occupied right up to the 19th century. It consists of a well-preserved tower and 17th century bawn where there is a plaque in memory of those members of the Boleyn family exiled here after the execution of Anne Boleyn, wife of Henry VIII.

CLONALIS HOUSE *Castlerea, County Roscommon*   9 F4

In the town that was the birthplace of Oscar Wilde's father, William Wilde, the noted antiquary, Clonalis House is the 19th century version of what was once the seat of O'Conor Don, of the O'Conors of Connacht, who produced two 12th century kings of Ireland. The house is a museum devoted to the family's colourful history.

CLONMACNOIS MONASTERY *County Offaly*   15 F2

Sitting on a ridge on the banks of the Shannon, the remains of one of Ireland's first and most holy monasteries would ideally be approached by boat from Athlone. Founded in 545 by St Kiaran, a few months before his death, his tomb became an object of pilgrimage and the monastery grew to become a centre of Irish art and literature. The burial place of several Kings of Tara and Connacht, Clonmacnois has endured many fires and numerous pillagings by Irish, Viking and English. The remains consist of two fine High Crosses, 400 memorial slabs from the 8th,

9th and 10th centuries, two Round Towers and eight churches. The 10th century West cross, with its frieze depicting St Kiaran and the local king from whom he obtained the monastery land, and the magnificently carved doorway of the Cathedral church are of particular interest.

CONG ABBEY *County Mayo*   9 D4

Although the village is best known nowadays for the impressive mock medieval castle of Ashford, now a hotel, that was built for Sir Arthur Guinness, in Irish history Cong is associated with its monastery founded in the 6th century by St Feichin. This was superseded by an Augustinian monastery in the 12th century of which the inscribed base of a cross remains in the main street, whilst the remains of the chancel of the abbey church are to be found outside the village to the southwest. It has a beautiful north door but most appealing of all are the three doorways in the remaining convent buildings, thse contain some of the finest medieval Irish carving in existence.

CRAG CAVE *County Kerry*   19 D4

Not far from Tralee, Crag Cave is really a network of limestone caves some 2.5 miles in length, discovered only in 1983. Over a million years old, they are festooned with stalactites and stalagmites, many of which have conjoined to form curtains and pillars. The Crystal Gallery is so called because of the white straw stalactites that glitter in the light.

DONEGAL CASTLE *Donegal, County Donegal*   4 C4

The late 15th century castle is just off the main square of this market town that has given its name to the county. Originally the seat of the O'Donnells, the castle tower was built by Red Hugh II O Donnell in 1505, whilst additions, including the magnificent fireplace in the banqueting hall, were made in the 17th century by a later occupant, the Planter Sir Basil Brooke, who was responsible for the fine Jacobean fortified house that forms part of the castle.

DUBLIN BOTANIC GARDENS *Dublin* 16 E2

Dublin's Botanic Gardens, in the suburb of Glasnevin, beyond the Royal Canal, were created in 1795 by the Royal Dublin Society, passing to the state in 1878. In its 50 acres there are several notable conservatories including one, over 400 ft in length, by Richard Turner who also designed for Kew in London. One of the finest botanical gardens in Europe, it is especially noted for its conifers, cycads, herbaceous borders and orchids, and boasts a lily pond, a sunken garden and a rock garden.

DUBLIN CASTLE *Dublin, County Dublin* 26 B2

Built at the turn of the 13th century, Dublin Castle has been a gaol for many important characters throughout Irish history, as well as the seat of English power until 1922. Nonetheless, it has never had to withstand a serious assault. Its only real enemy was neglect and the whole edifice was more or less reconstructed throughout the 18th century; and although it still retains an air of fortified unity, the only substantial medievalremains are the southeast or Record tower and the layout of the Upper Castle Yard. The original moat has also been discovered.The 18th century work was the last major brick construction in Dublin and guided tours will take you through the magnificently decorated and furnished State Apartments which include St Patrick's Hall (where Irish presidents are inaugurated), the circular Supper Room in the handsome Bermingham Tower, and the Throne Room. In the Lower Castle Yard is the impressive Church of the Most Holy Trinity, or the Chapel Royal, in Gothick style.

DUBLIN CATHEDRAL *Dublin* 26 B3

St Patrick's Cathedral is the largest church in Ireland and has for much of its existence had to compete with Christchurch for its Cathedral status. Founded in 1191 and rebuilt in the 14th century it is essentially Early English in style, although damage wrought during the Cromwellian wars was only restored in the 1860s. The satirist Jonathan Swift, Dean of the Cathedral 1713-45, is buried here.The baptistry, paved with 13th century tiles, is all that remains of the first church, whilst at the west end of the nave stands the old Chapter House door. The best preserved part of the medieval church, however, is the Choir which came to be the chapel of the now defunct Order of St Patrick, instituted in 1783. Among the monuments perhaps the most impressive is the Boyle Monument, erected by the Earl of Cork in memory of his wife Catherine.

DUN AENGUS FORT *Inishmore, Aran Islands, County Galway*   **14 B3**

Towards the far southwestern part of the island, on a spectacularly desolate slope overlooking the Atlantic, are the scattered remains of Dun Aengus (or, according to the most correct pronunciation, Doon Eeneece), one of the most important prehistoric forts in Europe, some 2500 years old. The 11 acre site consists of three enclosures with dry-stone walls up to 18 feet high. Most striking is the arrangement of jagged limestone menhirs which defend the middle wall.

DUNLUCE CASTLE (or Mermaid's Castle) *County Antrim*   **6 C2**

Just northwest of the town of Bushmills, famous for its whiskey distillery, Dunluce Castle is dramatically situated on a high rock overlooking the sea. It was first a Macquillan stronghold, then came to the MacDonnells until the 17th century when the occupied domestic quarters fell into the sea. The earliest part dates back to the late 13th century whilst the other sections - the Scottish gatehouse, the loggia - were built at different times up to the 17th century.

DUNSOGHLY CASTLE *Finglas, County Dublin*   **17 E2**

Just three miles to the northwest of Finglas, Dunsoghly Castle consists of a stately residential keep-like tower on three floors buttressed by rectangular corner turrets. It was built in the 15th century by Thomas Plunkett, Chief Justice of the King's Bench, whilst the nearby chapel was built in 1573 by Sir John Plunkett, also Chief Justice but for the Queen's Bench.

FOTA HOUSE *Carrigtwohill, County Cork*   **20 A4**

Fota House is on Fota Island which, accessible by causeways, sits in the River Lee Estuary. Built in 1820 for the Earls of Barrymore, it is a handsome Regency house with a fine collection of 18th and 19th century furniture and Irish landscape paintings. In the surrounding grounds is the internationally renowned arboretum begun in the 1820s with its collections of rare shrubs and semi-tropical and coniferous trees, which has so far escaped a threatened tourist development. There is also a wildlife park and bee garden.

GALLURUS ORATORY *nr. Ballyferriter, County Kerry* 18 A4

On the beautiful Dingle peninsula, at Lateevmore, which is about 2 miles east of Ballyferriter, is Gallarus oratory, a corbel-roofed dry-stone structure of remarkable perfection and completely waterproof. A Christian chapel that is over one thousand years old, it lacks only the crosses that once decorated the roof.

GLIN CASTLE *County Limerick* 19 D2

The village of Glin lies on the south shore of the Shannon Estuary. The Fitzgeralds, Knight of Glin, have lived here for over 700 years, first in a castle in the village itself, of which a fragment still remains; and then in Glin Castle, a Georgian-Gothick construction to the west of the village which dates from 1770 and which is still occupied by the family. Set in charming gardens, the house is decorated with fine plasterwork and hung with an interesting painting collection.

GRIANAN OF AILEACH *County Donegal* 5 E2

Five miles northeast of Newtowncunningham, on Greenan Mountain, this fort consists of a huge cashel (stone fort), probably dating from the early Christian period, standing at the centre of a series of three earthen banks covering 4 acres, which are either late Bronze or early Iron Age. An important stronghold of the Christian kingdom of Aileach, it retained a mythological importance long after its strategic value had passed away. There are, however, still wonderful views across the Foyle and Swilly.

HOWTH CASTLE GARDENS *Howth, County Dublin* 17 E2

Ten miles to the northeast of Dublin, Howth is a fishing port and resort. Howth Castle has been the seat of the Lawrence family since the 16th century although the family had settled in the area some 400 years previously. The castle (private) dates from 1564 and the beautiful gardens, for which soil had to be brought by the sackful by the castle staff in 1850, are renowned for their azaleas, and 2000 varieties of rhododendrons.

JAPANESE GARDENS *Tully, County Kildare*   16 C3

In the grounds of the National Stud at Tully, a short distance east of Kildare Town, the Japanese Gardens were planted by the Japanese gardener, Eida, and his son Minoru, between 1906 and 1910. Symbolising the ages of man from birth to death, the route takes you from the Gate of Oblivion and the Cave of Birth to the Garden of Eternity via the Hill of Ambition and the Well of Ambition. The Zen Meditation Garden was added in 1976.

KELLS PRIORY *County Kilkenny*   20 C2

In 1193 a priory was founded in Kells for Canons Regular of St Augustine from Bodmin in Cornwall. The impressive remains, 5 acres surrounded by substantial medieval fortified walls, with mostly complete 15th century dwelling towers, are divided into two courts by a branch of the river, in the northernmost of which are the remains of the church, with traces of medieval paving tiles, and the ruined claustral buildings.

KING JOHN'S CASTLE *Carlingford, County Louth*   12 C2

The small seaport of Carlingford, on the unspoilt Cooley Peninsula, is located at the foot of the 1935 foot Slieve Foye, overlooking Carlingford Lough. The castle remains, strategically located to command the quay, dating back to the late 12th century, played host to King John who stayed here on his way to attack Hugh de Lacy, at Carrickfergus. It has an unusual D-shape while the west gateway was designed to allow the entry of only one horseman at a time. The remains of an earlier castle include the southwest tower and the west wall.

KING JOHN'S CASTLE *Limerick, County Limerick*   19 F2

In the Old Town of Limerick (on a sort of island formed by the River Shannon and the River Abbey), the 13th century castle, the most formidable English stronghold in western Ireland, is a fine example of Norman fortified architecture. It has recently been partly converted into a museum which displays antique armaments (catapults and battering rams) and tells of the castle's role in Limerick's dramatic history.

KNOWTH TOMB *County Meath*   11 F4

Almost 2 miles to the northwest of the best known cairn at Newgrange, Knowth is another of the passage-tombs at the Bend of the Boyne. Built some 3000 years BC it is up to 50 ft high and 280 ft in diameter. Surrounded by a number of other, smaller cairns, the main cairn contains 2 tombs, the most westerly of which is 100 feet in length and different from the others in that it is lintelled and straighter; whilst the other is cruciform, with a corbelled roof. A quite considerable amount of ornamentation was discovered along with the cremated remains. It continued to be used up to the Iron Age when it seems also to have become a fortress.

LISMORE CASTLE GARDENS *Lismore, County Waterford*   20 B3

The castle, handsomely located above the Blackwater, was built in the 19th century by Joseph Paxton, architect of the Crystal Palace in London, for the 6th Duke of Devonshire, incorporating the remains of the medieval castle erected by Prince John of England in 1185. The castle (private) is partially surrounded by delightful walled gardens, with areas of woodland, shrubberies, and a Yew Walk. In spring the gardens are at their best when the camellias and magnolias are in flower. The Elizabethan poet Edmund Spenser is said to have composed part of the Faerie Queene in the grounds.

LISSADELL HOUSE *Raghly, County Sligo*   9 F1

Just over four miles outside the hamlet of Raghly which hangs off a promontory on the north side of Sligo Bay, Lissadell House, situated in conifer clad parkland overlooking the sea, was built in 19th century Classical style for the patriotic Gore-Booth family. The Arctic explorer Sir Henry Gore-Booth was born here, as were his daughters Eva, the poetess, and Constance, who became the first woman member of the

British House of Commons, but who chose to sit instead in the revolutionary Dail Eireann as minister for Labour. Refreshments are still served in the old-fashioned kitchen.

MARBLE ARCH CAVES *County Fermanagh* 10 C2

This system of caves, about 10 miles southwest of Enniskillen, has been formed by the action of 3 streams on a bed of Dartry limestone on 2,188 ft Mount Cuilcagh. Underground they converge to form a single river, the Cladagh, which flows via the 30ft limestone Marble Arch into Lough Macnean. The tour of the cave includes a boat ride on the underground lake and the presentation of an array of imaginatively illuminated and named rock formations, one of which, a stalactite, is over 7 feet long.

MELLIFONT ABBEY *County Louth* 12 B4

Four miles northwest of Drogheda, Mellifont was Ireland's first Cistercian abbey. Founded in 1140 by the King of Uriel, at the instigation of St Malachy, who had been inspired by St Bernard's work at Clairvaux, the abbey became the home of the Moore family after its suppression in 1539. Though scattered, the remains are of great interest and include portions of the Romanesque cloister arcade, the 13th century chapter house extension, and the octagonal washroom.

MONEA CASTLE *County Fermanagh* 10 C1

About 6 miles northwest of Enniskillen, Monea Castle was built in 1618 by the Rev. Malcolm Hamilton in Scottish Plantation style. It was burnt out in the 18th century but is in a reasonable state of preservation and its remaining two circular towers at the front and its crow-stepped gables add to its Scottish flavour.

MOUNT STEWART HOUSE *nr. Newtownards, County Down* 7 E4

The 18th century former seat of the Marquess of Londonderry, and childhood home of Lord Castlereagh, the 19th century British Prime Minister, now belongs to the National Trust. A severely Classical building, it sits amid 80 acres of gardens renowned for their many rare plants, trees and fanciful topiary. The Temple of the Winds, also in the grounds, is an exquisite banqueting hall built in 1785.

MOUNTUSHER GARDENS *Ashford, County Wicklow*   17 E4

Next to the village of Ashford, charmingly located by the River Vartry, the gardens of Mount Usher are made up of 20 acres planted with over 5000 species of flora. Including many sub-tropical plants, the naturalised gardens, laid out in 1868 by Edward Walpole, of a Dublin family of linen manufacturers, are famous for the Eucalyptus and Eucryphia collections and offer some fine woodland walks.

MURLOUGH *Newcastle, County Down*   13 D2

About two miles to the north of Newcastle is this area of sand dunes, some of which were formed over 5000 years ago, stretching from the Carrigs River and the shore of Dundrum Bay. A wild haven for all types of sea and water birds, it is also a place where wild flowers grow in profusion.

NAVAN FORT *County Armagh*   11 F1

A little way to the west of the town of Armagh, the remains at Navan are of an 18 acre hill fort, crowned by a ceremonial tumulus, which together form the last remains of the seat of Ulster kings between 350 BC and 332 AD. It is also the Emhain Macha, the legendary home of Cu Chulainn, one of the knights of Ulster mythology.

NESS WOOD COUNTRY PARK *County Londonderry*   6 A3

The 46 acres of woodland were originally dominated by oak trees but many other species were added from the 17th century. The highlight of Ness, however, is the spectacular 30 ft waterfall, part of the River Burntollet, which since the last Ice Age has also created a series of gorges and rapids through the metamorphic rock.

PARKE'S CASTLE *County Leitrim*   10 B2

On the banks of Lough Gill, in Kilmore, close to Dromahaire, Parkes Castle is a

Plantation castle in markedly Scottish style built in the 17th century on the site of an earlier castle. In a good state of preservation, its courtyard walls are fortified with picturesque towers and gatehouses and it played a key role in the war of 1641 - 52. There is a permanent exhibition about the area as well as an excellent audio visual show.

POWERSCOURT HOUSE *nr. Enniskerry, County Wicklow* **17 E3**

A disastrous fire in the 1970's has left only the shell of Powerscourt House, built in 1730 for Viscount Powerscourt by the Huguenot architect Richard Cassels and then enlarged and altered in the 19th century. Its mountain setting is magnificent, however, as are the gardens with their handsome 19th century terraces, Monkey Puzzle Avenue, and Japanese Garden, added in 1908. In the grounds, and approachable by a separate car entrance, is a spectacular 400 feet waterfall.

PROLEEK DOLMEN *County Louth* **12 B2**

To the north of Dundalk, the capital of Louth, in Aghnaskeagh, are two prehistoric cairns and a fort. Nearby Proleek is the site of the so called 'Giant's Load', a tomb that is the legendary grave of Para Bui Mor Mhac Seoidin, the Scottish giant who challenged Finn MacCool. A trio of smaller upright stones supporting a larger capstone, the tomb dates back 3000 BC. It is thought that the capstone was hauled into position by means of a vanished earthen ramp.

QUIN ABBEY *County Clare* **15 D4**

The village of Quin is noted for a Franciscan friary founded in the early 15th century, the first Observantine house in Ireland. The ruins, incorporating an earlier castle, are sufficiently well preserved to clearly demonstrate the layout of a medieval friary.

RING OF KERRY *County Kerry* **22 C1**

The Ring of Kerry is a famous circular scenic route of about 115 miles around the Iveragh Peninsula. Clearly it can begin at any point on the route but the town of Killarney is generally considered the gateway to the peninsula, even if the best section lies between Kenmare and Killorglin. The fine mountain and maritime scenery is a constant companion but the route passes through or near to a number of interesting places including Sneem, with its old Anglican church; the 2000 year fort at Staigue; Derrynane National Historic Park, the former home of Daniel O'Connell; the resort of Waterville; Coomakesta Pass; Valencia Island; Knocknadobar Mountain; Cahergall Fort; Leacanabuaile Fort; Rossbeigh Strand; Glenbeigh with its Bog Village Museum; and Lough Caragh and its views across to Macgillycuddy's Reeks. Whilst the principal route more or less follows the coast, some of the finest scenery is to be found along the unmarked roads running through the interior of the peninsula.

ROCK OF CASHEL *County Tipperary*   20 B2

One of the most spectacular sights in Ireland, the Rock of Cashel is a steep limestone outcrop surmounted by the ruins of the ancient capital of the Kings of Munster. According to legend, St Patrick baptised Corc the Third here; and Brian Boru, High King of Ireland, was crowned here in 977. In 1101 King Murtagh O'Brien donated the rock to the church after which it became the See of the Archbishopric of Munster. The ruins are extensive and fascinating. Cormac's Chapel, built in the 1130s in a style sometimes called Hiberno-Romanesque, contains a magnificent carved 11th century sarcophagus; whilst the carved Cross of St Patrick is set into the coronation stone of the Kings of Munster. The main cathedral is essentially 13th century and although it has suffered pillage and neglect, it remains a fine example of Irish Gothic. There are remarkable views across the surrounding countryside from the part of the cathedral known as the Castle, built to house the 15th century bishops.

ROCK OF DUNAMASE *County Laois*   16 B4

Close to Portlaoise, on the Stradbally road, a large ruined castle sits on top of this 150 ft rock, all that remains of what was a considerable fortress, destroyed in the Cromwellian wars. Through the marriage of the daughter of the King of Leinster, it had moved into Anglo Norman hands in the late 12th century, and was twice rebuilt, in 1250 and at the end of the 15th century. There are fine views to be had from the summit of the rock where the remains of the gatehouse, walls and 13th century keep are still in evidence.

RUSSBOROUGH HOUSE *Blessington, County Wicklow*   **17 D3**
One of Ireland's foremost Palladian houses was built for a Dublin brewer, Joseph Leeson, 1st Earl of Milltown, by Richard Cassels and Francis Bindon in the 1740s. A granite exterior conceals an interior coated in extravagant stucco work and bearing a fine painting collection.

ST. CANICE CATHEDRAL *Kilkenny City*   **20 C1**
The city actually takes its name from St Canice who founded a monastery here in the 6th century, upon the site of which stands the current cathedral. Much restored in the 19th century, it is the second largest medieval cathedral in Ireland. Inside is the finest display of burial monuments in the country whilst the high round tower adjacent to the cathedral is the only substantial relic from the monastery. The building is essentially 13th century and the oldest tomb is also from this period, although the oldest decipherable slab is that of Jose Kyteler, the father of Alice Kyteler, tried for witchcraft in 1323.

SCRABO *Newtownards, County Down*   **7 E4**
The landscape roundabout is dominated by Scrabo Hill, a layer of volcanic rock over a mound of sandstone dominates the landscape. It is crowned by Scrabo Tower, erected in 1857 in memory of the third Marquess of Londonderry. Built in saturnine dolerite, and sandstone, it now houses a museum about the surrounding countryside, some of which is made up of 19th century beech and mixed woodland. There are magnificent views across Strangford Lough.

STAIGUE STONE FORT *nr. Castlecove, County Kerry*   **22 B2**
Amid the beautiful scenery overlooking Kenmare Bay, Staigue is a stone 2500 year old ringfort made up of a 13 ft thick rampart divided into terraces and linked by a system of stairways.

THOOR BALLYLEE *County Galway* 15 D3

The 16th century tower of Ballylee Castle, the Thoor Ballylee of Yeat's poems, is 5 miles northeast of the market town of Gort. A charming ivy clad tower on the banks of the river, Ballylee was Yeat's home in the 1920s, where he wrote the volume of poems entitled The Tower. After he left in 1929 the tower became a ruin once more until its restoration as a Yeats Museum in 1965.

WESTPORT HOUSE *County Mayo* 9 D3

Adjacent to the pretty village of Westport, planned by James Wyatt for the Marquess of Sligo, the house, built in about 1730, is by Richard Cassels, with additions by Wyatt in 1778. The house, entered from the Quay, contains a mixture of antique silver and furniture and modern entertainment facilities, whilst in the demesne itself is an ornamental lake, created by controlling the tides of Clew Bay, and a miniature zoo.

INDEX TO PLACE NAMES

Name	Page	Grid
Aasleagh	8	C4
Abbey	15	E3
Abbeydorney	18	C3
Abbeyfeale	19	D3
Abbeyleix	16	B4
Abbeyshrule	10	C4
Abington	19	F2
Achill	8	C3
Achonry	9	F2
Aclare	9	E2
Adamstown	21	E2
Adare	19	E2
Adrigole	22	C3
Aghaboe	16	B4
Aghabullogue	23	E2
Aghadoon	8	B1
Aghadowry	10	C3
Aghagallon	12	C1
Aghagower	9	D4
Aghalee	7	D4
Aghamore	9	E3
Aghanloo	5	F2
Aghavannagh	17	D4
Aghaville	23	D3
Aghern	20	A3
Aghleam	8	B2
Aghnacliff	10	C3
Agivey	6	C2
Aglish, *Tipperary*	15	F4
Aglish, *Waterford*	20	B3
Agnagar Bridge	22	B2
Ahafona	18	C3
Ahakista	22	C3
Ahascragh	15	F2
Ahenny	20	C2
Aherla	23	E2
Ahoghill	6	C3
Aldergrove	7	D4
Allen	16	C3
Allenwood	16	C3
Allihies	22	B3
Altagowlan	10	B2
Anascaul	18	B4
Annacarty	20	A1
Annacotty	19	F2
Annagassan	11	F3
Annaghdown	15	D2
Annagry	4	C2
Annahilt	12	C1
Annalong	13	D2
Annamoe	17	E4
Annayalla	11	E2
Annestown	20	C3
Annsborough	13	D1
Antrim	7	D4
Araglin	20	A3
Ard	14	B2
Ardabrone	9	F2
Ardagh	19	E3
Ardanairy	17	E4
Ardara	4	B4
Ardattin	21	E1
Ardcath	11	F4
Ardconry	15	F4
Ardee	11	F3
Ardfert	18	C3
Ardfinnan	20	B2
Ardglass, *Cork*	20	A4
Ardglass, *Down*	13	D2
Ardgroom	22	C3
Ardkeen	13	D1
Ardlougher	10	C2
Ardmore, *Galway*	20	B4
Ardmore, *Londonderry*	14	B2
Ardmore, *Waterford*	5	F2
Ardnacrusha	19	F2
Ardnasodan	15	D2
Ardpatrick	19	F3
Ardrahan	15	D3
Ardscull	16	C4
Ardstraw	5	E4
Arghavas	10	C3
Arklow	17	E4
(An tinbhear Mór)		
Arless	16	C4
Armagh	11	F1
Armoy	6	C2
Arryheernabin	5	D1
Arthurstown	21	D3
Articlave	5	F2
Artigarvan	5	E3
Arvagh	10	C3
Ashbourne	17	D2
Ashford, *Limerick*	19	E3
Ashford, *Wicklow*	17	E4
Askeaton	19	E2
Askill	10	B1
Astee	18	C2
Athboy	11	E4
Athea	19	D3
Athenry	15	D2
Athlacca	19	F3
Athleague	10	B4
Athlone	16	A2
(Baile Átha Luain)		
Athy	16	C4
Attanagh	16	B4
Attavalley	8	C2
Attica	12	C2
Attymass	9	E2
Attymon	15	E2
Augbrim	15	D4
Aughamullan	6	C4
Augher	11	D1
Aughils Bridge	18	C4
Aughnacloy	11	E1
Aughnasheelan	10	C2
Aughrim, *Galway*	15	F2
Aughrim, *Wicklow*	17	E4
Aughris	9	E1
Aughrus More	8	B4
Avoca	17	E4
B		
Baillieborough	11	E3
Balbriggan	12	C4
Balla	9	E3
Ballaghaderreen	9	F3
Ballaghkeen	21	E2
Ballee	13	D1
Ballickmoyler	16	C4
Ballina	15	E4
Ballina (Béal an Átha)	9	D2
Ballinaboy	14	A2
Ballinadee	23	F3
Ballinafad	10	B2
Ballinagar	16	B3
Ballinagh	11	D3
Ballinagore	16	B2
Ballinakill	16	B4
Ballinalack	11	D4
Ballinalee	10	C4
Ballinamallard	10	C1
Ballinameen	10	B3
Ballinamore	10	C2
Ballinamuck	10	C3
Ballinamult	20	B3
Ballinascarthy	23	E3
Ballinasloe	15	F2
(Béal Átha na Sluaighe)		
Ballinclogher	18	C3
Ballincollig	23	F2
Ballincrea	21	D2
Ballinderreen	15	D3
Ballinderry, *Antrim*	7	D4
Ballinderry, *Tipperary*	15	F4
Ballindine	9	E4
Ballindooly	15	D2
Ballindrait	5	D3
Ballineen	23	E3
Ballingarry, *Limerick*	19	E3
Ballingarry, *Tipperary*	20	C1
Ballingeary	23	D2
Ballingurteen	23	E3
Ballinhassig	23	F3
Ballinleeny	19	E3
Ballinlough	9	F4
Ballinrobe	9	D4
Ballinruan	15	D4
Ballinskelligs	22	B2
Ballinspittle	23	F3
Ballintober, *Mayo*	9	D4
Ballintober, *Roscommon*	9	F4
Ballintoy	6	C2
Ballintra	4	C4
Ballinure	20	B1
Ballisodare	9	F2
Ballivor	16	C2
Ballon	21	D1
Ballure	10	B1
Ballyagran	19	E3
Ballybay	11	E2
Ballybofey	5	D3
Ballyboghil	17	E2
Ballybogy	6	C2
Ballybrack, *Dublin*	17	E3
Ballybrack, *Kerry*	22	B2
Ballybrittas	16	C3
Ballybroad	19	F2
Ballybrophy	16	A4
Ballybunnion	18	C3
Ballycahill	20	B1
Ballycallan	20	C1
Ballycanew	21	F1
Ballycarney	21	E1
Ballycarra	9	D3
Ballycarry	7	E3
Ballycastle, *Antrim*	7	D2
Ballycastle, *Mayo*	9	D1
Ballyclare	7	D4
Ballyclough	19	E4
Ballycolla	16	B4
Ballyconneely	14	A2
Ballyconnell, *Cavan*	10	C2
Ballyconnell, *Sligo*	9	F1
Ballycotton	20	A4
Ballycroy	8	C2
Ballycumber	16	A2
Ballydangan	15	F2
Ballydavid	15	E3
Ballydavis	16	B4
Ballydehob	23	D4
Ballydesmond	19	D4
Ballydonegan	22	B3
Ballyduff, *Kerry*	18	C3
Ballyduff, *Waterford*	20	A3
Ballyfarnagh	9	E3
Ballyfarnan	10	B2
Ballyfasy	21	D2
Ballyfeard	23	F3
Ballyferriter	18	A4
Ballyfin	16	B3
Ballyforan	15	F2
Ballyfore	16	C2
Ballygalley	7	E3

Name	Page	Grid	Name	Page	Grid	Name	Page	Grid
Ballygar	15	F2	Ballynoe, *Cork*	20	A4	Bellewstown	11	F4
Ballygarrett	21	F1	Ballynoe, *Down*	13	D1	Bellmount	16	A3
Ballygawley	11	E1	Ballynunty	20	B1	Belmullet	8	B2
Ballyglass, *Mayo*	9	D4	Ballynure	7	D3	Beltra, *Mayo*	9	D3
Ballyglass, *Mayo*	9	F3	Ballyporeen	20	A3	Beltra, *Sligo*	9	F2
Ballygorman	5	E1	Ballyquin	18	B4	Belturbet	11	D2
Ballygowan	13	D1	Ballyragget	20	C1	Belville	9	D2
Ballyhack	21	D3	Ballyroan	16	B4	Benburb	11	E1
Ballyhaght	19	F3	Ballyroddy	10	B3	Bennettsbridge	20	C1
Ballyhahill	19	D2	Ballyroebuck	21	E1	Beragh	5	E4
Ballyhaise	11	D2	Ballyronan	6	C4	Bessbrook	11	F2
Ballyhalbert	13	E1	Ballyroon	22	C4	Bettystown	12	C4
Ballyhale, *Galway*	15	D2	Ballyshannon	10	B1	Bindoo	5	E2
Ballyhale, *Kilkenny*	20	C2	Ballysimon	21	E2	Binghamstown	8	B2
Ballyhar	18	C4	Ballysteen	19	E2	Birdhill	19	F2
Ballyhaunis	9	E4	Ballytoohy	8	B3	Birr	16	A3
Ballyhean	9	D3	Ballytore	16	C4	Black Bull	17	D2
Ballyhear	9	E4	Ballyvaldon	21	F2	Blacklion	10	C1
Ballyheigue	18	C3	Ballyvaughan	14	C3	Blackrock	11	F3
Ballyhoe Bridge	6	C2	Ballyvoge	23	E2	Blacktown	5	D4
Ballyhooly	19	F4	Ballyvoneen	15	E2	Blackwater	21	F2
Ballyhornan	13	D1	Ballyvourney	23	E2	Blackwatertown	11	F1
Ballyjamesduff	11	D3	Ballyvoy	7	D2	Blanchardstown	17	D2
Ballykeeran	16	A2	Ballyvoyle	20	C3	Blaney	10	C1
Ballykelly	5	F2	Ballywalter	7	F4	Blarney	23	F2
Ballykilleen	16	C3	Ballyward	12	C1	Blennerville	18	C4
Ballylanders	19	F3	Ballywilliam	21	D2	Blessington	17	D3
Ballylaneen	20	C3	Balnamore	6	C2	Blue Ball	16	A3
Ballyleague	10	B4	Balrath	11	F4	Blueford	19	E4
Ballyleny	11	F1	Balrothey	12	C4	Bodoney	11	D1
Ballylickey	23	D3	Baltimore	23	D4	Bodyke	15	E4
Ballyliffen	5	E1	Baltinglass	17	D4	Boher	19	F2
Ballylongford	19	D3	Baltray	12	C4	Boheraphuca	16	A4
Ballylynan	16	C4	Banada	9	E2	Boherboy	19	E4
Ballymacarbery	20	B3	Banagher	15	F3	Bohermeen	11	E4
Ballymacelligott	18	C4	Banbridge	12	C1	Boho	10	C1
Ballymack	20	C1	Bandon	23	F3	Bohola	9	E3
Ballymackilroy	11	E1	Bangor	7	E4	Bolea	5	F2
Ballymacmague	20	B3	Bangor Erris	8	C2	Boolteens	18	C4
Ballymacoda	20	B4	Bannow	21	D3	Boolyglass	20	C2
Ballymacurley	10	B4	Bansha	20	A2	Borris	21	D1
Ballymadog	20	B4	Banteer	19	E4	Borris-in-Ossory	16	A4
Ballymagaraghy	5	F1	Bantry	23	D3	Borrisokane	15	F4
Ballymagorry	5	E3	Barefield	15	D4	Borrisoleigh	20	A1
Ballymahon	10	C4	Barna	14	C3	Boston	15	D4
Ballymakeery	23	E2	Barnacahoge	9	E3	Bottlehill	23	F2
Ballymakenny	11	F4	Barnaderg	15	E2	Boviel	5	F3
Ballymartin	12	C2	Barnatra	8	C2	Boyle	10	B3
Ballymena	7	D3	Barneycarroll	9	E4	Brackagh	16	B3
Ballymoe	9	F4	Barnmeen	12	C2	Brackloon	9	F3
Ballymoney	6	C2	Barraduff	19	D4	Bracknagh	16	C3
Ballymore, *Donegal*	5	D2	Barry	10	C4	Brandon	18	B4
Ballymore, *Westmeath*	16	A2	Bawn Cross Roads	19	E4	Bray (Bré)	17	E3
Ballymore Eustace	17	D3	Bawnard	20	A4	Breaghva	18	C2
Ballymorris	20	C3	Bawnboy	10	C2	Breen	21	E2
Ballymote	9	F2	Beagh	9	E4	Brickeens	9	E4
Ballymurphy	21	D1	Beal	18	C2	Brideswell	15	F2
Ballymurry	10	B4	Bealaclugga	15	D3	Bridgeland	17	D4
Ballynabola	21	D2	Bealalaw Bridge	22	C2	Bridgend	5	E2
Ballynacallagh	22	B3	Bealnablath	23	E3	Bridgetown, *Donegal*	4	C4
Ballynacally	19	E2	Beaufort	18	C4	Bridgetown, *Wexford*	21	E3
Ballynacarriga	23	E3	Bekan	9	E4	Brinlack	4	C2
Ballynacarrigy	11	D4	Belclare	15	D2	Brittas	17	D3
Ballynafid	11	D4	Belcoo	10	C1	Brittas Bay	17	E4
Ballynagree	23	E2	Belderg	9	D1	Britway	20	A4
Ballynahinch, *Down*	13	D1	Belfast	7	D4	Broadford, *Clare*	19	F1
Ballynahinch, *Galway*	14	B2	Belfast Airport	7	D4	Broadford, *Limerick*	19	E3
Ballynahowen	16	A2	Belgooly	23	F3	Broadway	21	F3
Ballynakill, *Carlow*	21	D1	Bellacorick	8	C2	Brookeborough	11	D1
Ballynakill, *Westmeath*	16	A2	Bellaghy	6	C3	Broomfield	11	F2
Ballynakilla	22	C3	Bellahy	9	E3	Brosna, *Kerry*	19	D3
Ballynamona	19	F4	Bellanagare	9	F3	Brosna, *Offaly*	16	A4
Ballynare	17	D2	Bellanaleck	10	C1	Broughal	16	A3
Ballynaskreena	18	C3	Bellanamore	4	C3	Broughderg	5	F4
Ballynastraw	21	E2	Bellaneeny	15	F2	Broughshane	7	D3
Ballyneaner	5	E3	Bellavary	9	E3	Brownstown	21	D3
Ballyneety	19	F2	Belleek, *Armagh*	11	F2	Bruff	19	F3
Ballynockan	17	D3	Belleek, *Fermanagh*	10	B1	Bruree	19	F3

Name	Page	Grid
Buckna	7	D3
Buckode	10	B1
Bullaun	15	E3
Bunacurry	8	B3
Bunalty	8	C2
Bunbeg	4	C2
Bunclody	21	E1
Buncrana	5	E2
Bundoran	10	B1
Bunlahy	10	C3
Bunmahon	20	C3
Bunnaglass	15	E3
Bunnahowen	8	C2
Bunnanadden	9	F2
Bunnyconnellan	9	E2
Burnchurch	20	C1
Burnfoot, Cork	19	F4
Burnfoot, Donegal	5	E2
Burnfoot, Londonderry	5	F3
Burren, Down	12	C2
Burren, Mayo	9	D3
Burron	15	D3
Burtonport	4	B3
Bushmills	6	C2
Butlers Bridge	11	D2
Butlerstown	23	F3
Buttevant	19	F4

C

Name	Page	Grid
Cadamstown	16	A3
Caddy	6	C3
Caher	15	E4
Caherbarnagh	23	E2
Caherconlish	19	F2
Cahermore, Cork	22	B3
Cahermore, Galway	15	D3
Cahir	20	B2
Cahirciveen	22	B2
Caledon	11	E1
Callan	20	C2
Caltra	15	E2
Caltraghlea	15	F2
Calverstown	16	C3
Camaross	21	E2
Camolin	21	E1
Camp	18	C4
Campile	21	D3
Canningstown	11	E3
Cappagh, Limerick	19	E2
Cappagh, Tyrone	5	F4
Cappaghmore	15	D3
Cappalinnan	16	A4
Cappamore	19	F2
Cappataggle	15	E3
Cappawhite	20	A1
Cappoquin	20	B3
Caraunkeelwy	15	D2
Carbury	16	C2
Carland	5	F4
Carlanstown	11	E4
Carlingford	12	C2
Carlow (Ceatharlach)	16	C4
Carna	14	B2
Carnagh	11	F2
Carnanreagh	5	E3
Carndonagh	5	E2
Carnduff	7	D2
Carnew	21	E1
Carney	9	F1
Carnlough	7	D3
Carnmore	15	D2
Carnteel	11	E1
Carracastle	9	F3
Carragh	17	D3
Carraloe	14	B3
Carran	15	D4
Carrick, Donegal	4	B4
Carrick, Wexford	21	E3
Carrick-on-Shannon	10	B3
Carrick-on-Suir (Carraig na Siuire)	20	C2
Carrickaboy	11	D3
Carrickbeg	20	C2
Carrickboy	10	C4
Carrickfergus	7	E4
Carrickmacross	11	F3
Carrickmore	5	F4
Carrig	15	F3
Carrigaholt	18	C2
Carrigaline	23	F3
Carrigallen	10	C3
Carriganimmy	23	E2
Carrigans	5	E3
Carrigart	5	D2
Carrigkerry	19	D3
Carrigtwohill	20	A4
Carrowdore	7	E4
Carrowkeel, Donegal	5	E2
Carrowkeel, Galway	15	E3
Carrowkennedy	9	D4
Carrowmore, Galway	15	D3
Carrowmore, Sligo	9	F2
Carrowneden	9	F2
Carrownurlar	9	F3
Carryduff	7	E4
Cashel, Donegal	5	D2
Cashel, Galway	14	B2
Cashel, Galway	9	F4
Cashel, Laois	16	B4
Cashel, Tipperary	20	B2
Cashelgarran	9	F1
Cashla	15	D2
Cashleen	8	B4
Castlebar (Calseán an Bharraigh)	9	D3
Castlebellingham	11	F3
Castleblakeney	15	E2
Castleblayney	11	E2
Castlebridge	21	E2
Castlecaufield	11	E1
Castlecomer	16	B4
Castleconnell	19	F2
Castleconor	9	E2
Castlecor	19	E4
Castlecove	22	B3
Castledawson	6	C3
Castlederg	5	D4
Castledermot	16	C4
Castleellis	21	E2
Castlefinn	5	D3
Castlefreke	23	E4
Castlegal	9	F1
Castlegregory	18	B4
Castlehill	9	D2
Castleisland	19	D4
Castlejordan	16	C2
Castlelyons	20	A3
Castlemaine	18	C4
Castlemartyr	20	A4
Castleplunket	10	B4
Castlepollard	11	D4
Castlerea	9	F4
Castlereagh	7	E4
Castlerock	5	F2
Castleroe	6	C2
Castletown, Clare	15	D4
Castletown, Cork	23	E3
Castletown, Laois	16	B4
Castletown, Meath	11	F4
Castletown, Westmeath	11	D4
Castletown, Wexford	21	F1
Castletown Bere	22	C3
Castletown Geoghegan	16	B2
Castletownroche	19	F4
Castletownshend	23	E4
Castleville	9	E4
Castlewarren	21	D1
Castlewellan	12	C2
Catherdaniel	22	B3
Causeway	18	C3
Causeway Head	6	C2
Cavan	11	D3
Cavanagarven	11	E2
Celbridge	17	D2
Chapeltown, Antrim	7	D3
Chapeltown, Kerry	22	A2
Charlemont	11	F1
Charlestown	9	E3
Cheekpoint	21	D3
Church Hill	5	D3
Churchtown, Cork	20	A4
Churchtown, Cork	19	E4
Churchtown, Down	13	D1
Churchtown, Wexford	21	D3
Churchtown, Wexford	21	F3
Clady, Londonderry	6	C3
Clady, Tyrone	5	E3
Claggan	8	C3
Clanabogan	5	E4
Clane	17	D2
Clara	16	A2
Clarecastle	15	D4
Clareen	16	A3
Claregatway	15	D2
Claremorris	9	E4
Clarinbridge	15	D3
Clashmore	20	B4
Claudy	5	E3
Cleady	23	D2
Cleggan	8	B4
Clifden	14	A2
Clifferna	11	D3
Cliffonoy	9	F1
Clogh, Antrim	7	D3
Clogh, Kilkenny	16	B4
Clogh, Laois	16	B4
Clogh, Wexford	21	F1
Clogh Mills	6	C2
Cloghan, Donegal	5	D3
Cloghan, Offaly	16	A3
Cloghan, Westmeath	11	D4
Cloghane	18	B4
Cloghboy	4	B3
Cloghbrack	11	E4
Clogheen	20	B3
Clogher, Mayo	9	D3
Clogher, Tyrone	11	D1
Clogherhead	12	C3
Cloghy	13	E1
Clohamon	21	E1
Clohernagh	21	D3
Clonakenny	16	A4
Clonakilty	23	E3
Clonare	16	C2
Clonaslee	16	B3
Clonbern	9	F4
Clonbulloge	16	C3
Clonbur	9	D4
Cloncullen	16	A2
Clondalkin	17	D2
Clondulane	20	A3
Clonea	20	C3
Clonee	17	D2
Cloneen	20	B2
Clonegal	21	E1
Clones	11	D2
Clonfert	15	F3
Clonmany	5	E1
Clonmel (Cluain Meala)	20	B2
Clonmellon	11	E4
Clonmore, Carlow	17	D4
Clonmore, Tipperary	16	A4
Clonopy	16	A3
Clonoulty	20	A1

Name	Page	Grid	Name	Page	Grid	Name	Page	Grid
Clonroche	21	E2	Craigavon	11	F1	Cushina	16	B3
Clontarf	17	E2	Craigs	6	C3			
Clontibret	11	E2	Craigue	16	C4	**D**		
Clonygowan	16	B3	Cranagh	5	F3	Daingean	16	B2
Cloonacool	9	E2	Cranford	5	D2	Dalkey	17	E3
Cloonagh	11	D3	Cranny	19	D2	Dalystown	15	E3
Cloonbannin	19	E4	Cratloe	19	E2	Damastown	12	C4
Cloonboo	15	D2	Craughwell	15	E3	Damerstown	20	C1
Cloone	10	C3	Crawfordsburn	7	E4	Damhead	6	C2
Clooneagh	10	C3	Creagh, *Cork*	23	D4	Danesfort	10	C4
Cloonfad, *Roscommon*	9	F4	Creagh, *Fermanagh*	11	D1	Darby's Bridge	22	B2
Cloonfad, *Roscommon*	15	F3	Crean's Cross Roads	23	E2	Darkley	11	F2
Cloonkeen	9	D3	Crecora	19	F2	Darragh	19	E2
Cloonlara	19	F2	Creegh	19	D2	Davidstown	21	E2
Cloontia	9	F3	Creeslough	5	D2	Delgany	17	E3
Clough	13	D1	Creevagh	9	D2	Delvin	11	E4
Cloughjordan	15	F4	Creggan, *Armagh*	11	F2	Dernagree	19	E4
Cloughmore	8	C3	Creggan, *Tyrone*	5	F4	Derreen	9	D3
Cloyfin	6	C2	Cregganbaun	8	C4	Derreendaragh	22	C2
Cloyne	20	A4	Creggs	9	F4	Derreeny Bridge	23	D3
Clynacartan	22	A2	Crilly	11	E1	Derry	10	B2
Coachford	23	F2	Crinkill	16	A3	Derrybeg	4	C2
Coagh	6	C4	Croagh, *Donegal*	4	C4	Derrybrien	15	E3
Coalisland	6	C4	Croagh, *Limerick*	19	E3	Derrydruel	4	C3
Cobh (An Cóbh)	20	A4	Crockets Town	9	E2	Derryerglinna	14	C2
Coblinstown	17	D4	Crockmore	5	D4	Derrygonnelly	10	C1
Coleraine	6	C2	Croghan, *Offaly*	16	B2	Derrygoolin	15	E4
Collgreane	10	B2	Croghan, *Roscommon*	10	B3	Derrylea	14	B2
Collon	11	F4	Crolly	4	C2	Derrylin	10	C2
Collooney	9	F2	Cromane	18	B4	Derrymore	18	C4
Collorus	22	C3	Crookedwood	11	D4	Derrynacreeve	10	C2
Colmanstown	15	E2	Crookhaven	22	C4	Derrynawilt	11	D2
Comber	7	E4	Crookstown	23	E2	Derryneen	14	B2
Commeen	4	C3	Croom	19	F3	Derryrush	14	B2
Cong	9	D4	Cross	9	D4	Derrytrasna	11	F1
Conlig	7	E4	Cross Barry	23	F3	Derrywode	9	F4
Connolly	14	C4	Cross Keys, *Meath*	11	E4	Dervock	6	C2
Connor	7	D3	Cross Keys, *Meath*	17	D2	Desertmartin	6	C3
Convoy	5	D3	Crossakeel	11	E4	Dingle	18	B4
Cookstown	5	F4	Crossdoney	11	D3	Doagh, *Antrim*	7	D4
Coola	9	F2	Crosserlough	11	D3	Doagh, *Donegal*	5	D2
Coolaney	9	F2	Crossgar	13	D1	Doagh Beg	5	D1
Coolattin	21	E1	Crossgare	6	C2	Dolla	20	A1
Coolbaun	15	F4	Crosshaven	20	A4	Donabate	17	E2
Coole	11	D4	Crosskeys	16	C3	Donadea	17	D2
Coolgrange	21	D1	Crossmaglen	11	F2	Donagh	11	D2
Coolgreany	21	F1	Crossmolina	9	D2	Donaghadee	7	E4
Coolmeen	19	D2	Crossna	10	B3	Donaghcloney	12	C1
Coolmore	4	C4	Crosspatrick, *Kilkenny*	20	B1	Donaghmore, *Laois*	16	A4
Coolock	17	E2	Crosspatrick, *Wicklow*	21	E1	Donaghmore, *Meath*	17	D2
Coolrain	16	A4	Crove	4	B4	Donaghmore, *Tyrone*	5	F4
Coolroebeg	21	D2	Crumlin	7	D4	Donard	17	D4
Cooneen	11	D1	Crusheen	15	D4	Donegal	4	C4
Cooraclare	19	D2	Cuilmore	8	C4	Doneraile	19	F4
Cootehill	11	E2	Culdaff	5	E1	Donohill	20	A2
Coppeen	23	E3	Culkey	10	C1	Donoughmore	23	F2
Coralstown	16	B2	Cullahill	16	B4	Dooagh	8	B3
Corbally	9	E2	Cullane	19	F3	Doobehy	9	D2
Corclogh	8	B2	Cullaville	11	F2	Doocastle	9	F3
Cordal	19	D4	Culleens	9	E2	Doochary	4	C3
Cordarragh	9	D4	Cullen	20	A2	Dooega	8	B3
Cork (Corcaigh)	23	F2	Cullin	9	E3	Dooghbeg	8	C3
Cork Airport	23	F2	Cullybackey	6	C3	Doogort	8	B3
Corkey	6	C2	Cullyhanna	11	F2	Doohooma	8	C2
Corlea	10	C4	Culmore	5	E2	Dooish	5	E4
Corlee	9	E3	Cummer	15	D2	Doon	20	A1
Cornamona	14	C2	Curracloe	21	E2	Doona	8	C2
Corofin	15	D3	Curragh	16	C3	Doonaha	18	C2
Corraleehan	10	C2	Curragh West	9	F4	Doonbeg	18	C2
Corraun	8	C3	Curraghroe	10	B4	Doonloughan	14	A2
Corry	10	B2	Curraglass	20	A3	Doonmanagh	18	B4
Costelloe	14	B2	Curran	6	C3	Douglas	23	F2
Courtmacsherry	23	F3	Curraun	14	C2	Douglas Bridge	5	E4
Courtown	21	F1	Curreeny	20	A1	Downhill	5	F2
Craanford	21	E1	Curry	9	E3	Downpatrick	13	D1
Craig	5	E3	Curryglass	22	C3	Dowra	10	B2
Craigantlet	7	E4	Cushendall	7	D2	Drangan	20	B2
Craigavad	7	E4	Cushendun	7	D2	Draperstown	5	F3

Name			Name			Name		
Dreenagh	18	B3	Dungourney	20	A4	Fews	20	C3
Drimmo	16	B4	Duniry	15	E3	Feystown	7	D3
Drimoleague	23	D3	Dunkerrin	16	A4	Fiddown	20	C2
Drinagh	23	E3	Dunkineely	4	B4	Finnea	11	D4
Dripsey	23	F2	Dunkitt	21	D3	Finny	9	D4
Drogheda (Droichead Átha)	11	F4	Dunlavin	17	D3	Fintona	11	D1
Droichead Nua (Newbridge)	16	C3	Dunleer	11	F3	Fintown	4	C3
Drom	20	B1	Dunlewy	4	C2	Finuge	18	C3
Dromahair	10	B2	Dunloy	6	C2	Finvoy	6	C2
Dromara	12	C1	Dunmanus	22	C4	Fivemiletown	11	D1
Dromard	9	F2	Dunmanway	23	E3	Flagmount	15	E4
Dromin	11	F3	Dunmoon	20	B4	Fontstown	16	C3
Dromina	19	E3	Dunmore	9	F4	Ford	21	F2
Dromineer	15	F4	Dunmore East	21	D3	Fordstown	11	E4
Dromiskin	11	F3	Dunmurry	7	D4	Forkhill	11	F2
Drommahane	19	F4	Dunnamaggan	20	C2	Formoyle	14	C3
Dromod	10	C3	Dunnamanagh	5	E3	Fort Stewart	5	D2
Dromore, *Down*	12	C1	Dunnamore	5	F4	Foulkesmill	21	E2
Dromore, *Tyrone*	11	D1	Dunquin	18	A4	Fountain Cross	15	D4
Dromore West	9	E2	Dunseverick	6	C2	Four Mile House	10	B4
Droom	23	D2	Dunshaughlin	17	D2	Foxford	9	E3
Drum	11	D2	Durrow, *Laois*	16	B4	Foygh	10	C4
Drumahoe	5	E3	Durrow, *Offaly*	16	B2	Foynes	19	E2
Drumandoora	15	E4	Durrus	23	D3	Freemount	19	E4
Drumanespick	11	E3	Dyan	11	E1	Frenchpark	9	F3
Drumaness	13	D1				Freshford	20	C1
Drumatober	15	E3	**E**			Furraleigh	20	C3
Drumbane	20	A1	Easky	9	E1			
Drumbilla	11	F2	Eden	7	E4	**G**		
Drumcard	10	C2	Edenderry	16	C2	Gainestown	16	B2
Drumcliff	9	F1	Ederny	5	D4	Galbally, *Limerick*	20	A2
Drumcollogher	19	E3	Edgeworthstown	10	C4	Galbally, *Wexford*	21	E2
Drumcondra	17	E2	Edmondstown	9	F3	Galmoy	20	B1
Drumconrath	11	F3	Eglinton	5	E2	Galros	16	A3
Drumcree	11	D4	Eglish	11	E1	Galway (Gaillimh)	15	D3
Drumduff	10	C1	Elphin	10	B3	Garadice	17	D2
Drumfea	21	D1	Elton	19	F3	Garlowcross	11	F4
Drumfree	5	E2	Emly	19	F3	Garnish	22	B3
Drumkeeran	10	B2	Emmoo	10	B4	Garr	16	B2
Drumlea	10	C3	Emyvale	11	E1	Garrane	23	E2
Drumlegagh	5	E4	Enfield	16	C2	Garranlahan	9	F4
Drumlish	10	C3	Ennis (Inis)	15	D4	Garrison	10	B1
Drummin	21	D2	Enniscorthy (Inis Córthaidh)	21	E2	Garristown	11	F4
Drummulin	10	B3	Enniskean	23	E3	Garrivinnagh	14	B2
Drumnacross	5	D3	Enniskerry	17	E3	Garronpoint	7	D2
Drumnakilly	5	E4	Enniskillen	10	C1	Garryvoe	20	A4
Drumone	11	D4	Ennistymon	14	C4	Garvagh, *Leitrim*	10	C3
Drumquin	5	E4	Errill	16	A4	Garvagh, *Londonderry*	6	C3
Drumraney	16	A2	Ervey Cross Roads	5	E3	Garvaghy	11	D1
Drumshanbo	10	B2	Eshnadarragh	11	D1	Garvary	10	C1
Drumskinny	5	D4	Eskragh	11	D1	Gaybrook	16	B2
Drumsurn	5	F3	Eyeries	22	B3	Geashill	16	B3
Drung	11	D3	Eyrecourt	15	F3	Geevagh	10	B2
Duagh	19	D3				Gerahies	22	C3
Dually	20	B2	**F**			Gilford	11	F1
Dublin (Baile Átha Cliath)	17	E2	Fahamore	18	B3	Glandore	23	E4
Dublin Airport	17	E2	Fahan	5	E2	Glanmire	23	F2
Duleek	11	F4	Falcarragh	4	C2	Glanworth	19	F4
Dún Laoghaire	17	E2	Fallmore	8	B2	Glarryford	6	C3
Dunaff	5	E1	Fanore	14	C3	Glaslough	11	E1
Dunbell	21	D1	Fardrum	16	A2	Glassan	16	A2
Dunboyne	17	D2	Farranfore	18	C4	Glenade	10	B1
Duncannon	21	D3	Feakle	15	E4	Glenamaddy	9	F4
Duncannon Bridge	19	D4	Fedamore	19	F3	Glenamoy	8	C2
Duncormick	21	E3	Feeard	18	C2	Glenariff	7	D2
Dundalk (Dún Dealgan)	11	F2	Feeny	5	F3	Glenarm	7	D3
Dunderry	11	E4	Fenagh, *Carlow*	21	D1	Glenavy	7	D4
Dundonald	7	E4	Fenagh, *Leitrim*	10	C3	Glenbeigh	18	B4
Dundrod	7	D4	Fenit	18	C4	Glencolumbkille	4	B4
Dundrum, *Down*	13	D2	Feohanagh	18	A4	Glencullen	17	E3
Dundrum, *Dublin*	17	E3	Feonanagh	19	E3	Glendowan	4	C3
Dundrum, *Tipperary*	20	A1	Ferbane	16	A3	Glendree	15	E4
Dunfanaghy	4	C2	Fermoy	20	A3	Glenduff	20	A3
Dungannon	11	E1	Ferns	21	E1	Glenealy	17	E4
Dungarvan	21	D1	Ferrybank	17	E4	Gleneely, *Donegal*	5	E2
Dungarvan (Dún Garbhán)	20	B3	Ferrycarrig	21	E2	Gleneely, *Donegal*	5	D3
Dungiven	5	F3	Fethard, *Tipperary*	20	B2	Glengarriff	23	D3
Dungloe	4	B3	Fethard, *Wexford*	21	D3	Glengavlen	10	C2

Name	Page	Grid	Name	Page	Grid	Name	Page	Grid
Glenhead	5	F2	Hillsborough	12	C1	Kilcoigan	15	D3
Glenhull	5	F4	Hilltown	12	C2	Kilcolman	23	E3
Gleniff	9	F1	Hollyford	20	A1	Kilcommon	20	B2
Glenmore, *Clare*	19	D2	Hollymount	9	E4	Kilconnel	14	C4
Glenmore, *Kilkenny*	21	D2	Hollywood	17	D3	Kilconnell	15	E2
Glennagevlagh	8	C4	Holycross	20	B1	Kilconney	11	D2
Glenoe	7	E3	Holywell	10	C1	Kilcoole	17	E3
Glenties	4	C3	Holywood	7	E4	Kilcormac	16	A3
Glentogher	5	E2	Horseleap, *Galway*	15	E2	Kilcrohane	22	C3
Glenville	23	F2	Horseleap, *Westmeath*	16	A2	Kilcullen	17	D3
Glin	19	D2	Hospital	19	F3	Kilcummin, *Kerry*	19	D4
Glinsk	14	B2	Howth	17	E2	Kilcummin, *Mayo*	9	D1
Glounthaune	23	F2	Hurler's Cross	19	E2	Kildalkey	11	E4
Glynn, *Antrim*	7	E3				Kildare	16	C3
Glynn, *Carlow*	21	D2	**I**			Kildavin	21	E1
Gneevgullia	19	D4	Inagh	14	C4	Kildorrey	19	F4
Golden	20	A2	Inch, *Donegal*	5	E2	Kildress	5	F4
Goleen	22	C4	Inch, *Kerry*	18	B4	Kilfenora	14	C4
Goresbridge	21	D1	Inch, *Wexford*	21	F1	Kilfinnane	19	F3
Gorey	21	F1	Inchigeelagh	23	E2	Kilfinny	19	E3
Gormanstown	12	C4	Inistioge	21	D2	Kilflynn	18	C3
Gort	15	D3	Inniscrone	9	E2	Kilgarvan	23	D2
Gortaclare	5	E4	Innishannon	23	F3	Kilglass, *Galway*	15	F2
Gortahork	4	C2	Inniskeen	11	F3	Kilglass, *Roscommon*	10	B3
Gortavoy Bridge	5	F4	Inver	4	C4	Kilgobnet	22	C2
Gorteen, *Cavan*	11	D3	Inveran	14	C3	Kilgowan	16	C3
Gorteen, *Galway*	9	F4	Irishtown	9	E4	Kilkea	16	C4
Gorteen, *Kilkenny*	16	C4	Irvinestown	10	C1	Kilkee	18	C2
Gorteen, *Sligo*	9	F3				Kilkeel	12	C2
Gorteen, *Waterford*	20	B4	**J**			Kilkelly	9	E3
Gorteeny	15	E4	Jamestown, *Laois*	16	C3	Kilkenny	20	C1
Gortin	5	E4	Jamestown, *Leitrim*	10	B3	(Cill Chainnigh)		
Gortmore	14	B2	Johnstown, *Kilkenny*	20	C1	Kilkerrin	9	F4
Gortnagallon	7	D4	Johnstown, *Wicklow*	21	F1	Kilkieran	14	B2
Gortnasillagh	9	F4	Johnstown, *Wicklow*	17	E4	Kilkinamurry	12	C1
Gowran	21	D1	Johnstown Bridge	16	C2	Kilkinlea	19	D3
Gracehill	6	C3	Johnswell	20	C1	Kilkishen	15	D4
Graffy	4	C3	Jonesborough	11	F2	Kill, *Kildare*	17	D3
Graiguenamanagh	21	D2	Julianstown	12	C4	Kill, *Waterford*	20	C3
Granabeg	17	D3				Killabunane	23	D2
Granard	11	D4	**K**			Killadeas	10	C1
Graney	16	C4	Kanturk	19	E4	Killadoon	8	C4
Grange, *Kilkenny*	20	C1	Katesbridge	12	C1	Killadysert	19	E2
Grange, *Louth*	12	C3	Keadue	10	B2	Killagan Bridge	6	C2
Grange, *Sligo*	9	F1	Keady	11	F2	Killala	9	D2
Grange, *Waterford*	20	B4	Kealkill	23	D3	Killaloe	15	E4
Grangebellow	12	C3	Kearney	13	E1	Killamerry	20	C2
Grangeford	16	C4	Keel	8	B3	Killann	21	E2
Grannagh	15	D3	Keeloges	9	F4	Killard	18	C2
Gransha	12	C1	Keenagh, *Longford*	10	C4	Killarney (Cill Airne)	19	D4
Greagh	10	C3	Keenagh, *Mayo*	9	D2	Killarone	14	C2
Greenan	17	E4	Kells, *Antrim*	7	D3	Killaskillen	16	C2
Greenanstown	12	C4	Kells, *Kerry*	22	B2	Killavil	9	F3
Greencastle, *Donegal*	5	F2	Kells, *Kilkenny*	20	C2	Killavullen	19	F4
Greencastle, *Down*	12	C2	Kells, *Meath*	11	E4	Killeagh	23	F2
Greencastle, *Tyrone*	5	F4	(Ceanannus Mór)			Killeany	14	B3
Greenfield	14	C2	Kellysgrove	15	F3	Killedmond	21	D1
Greenisland	7	E4	Kenmare	23	D2	Killeenleagh	23	D3
Greenore	12	C2	Kerrykeel	5	D2	Killeevan	11	D2
Grevine	20	C1	Kesh, *Fermanagh*	5	D4	Killeigh	16	B3
Greyabbey	7	E4	Kesh, *Sligo*	9	F2	Killen	5	D4
Greystones	17	E3	Kilargue	10	B2	Killena	21	F1
Groomsport	7	E4	Kilbaha	18	C2	Killenaule	20	B1
Gubaveeny	10	B2	Kilbeggan	16	B2	Killerrig	16	C4
Gulladuff	6	C3	Kilbeheny	20	A3	Killeshandra	11	D3
Gurteen	15	E2	Kilberry, *Kildare*	16	C4	Killeter	5	D4
Gweedore	4	C2	Kilberry, *Meath*	11	F4	Killimer	19	D2
Gweensalia	8	C3	Kilbride, *Meath*	11	E4	Killimor	15	F3
Gyleen	20	A4	Kilbride, *Meath*	17	D2	Killinaboy	15	D4
			Kilbride, *Wicklow*	17	D3	Killinchy	13	D1
H			Kilbride, *Wicklow*	17	E4	Killinick	21	E3
Hacketstown	17	D4	Kilbrien	20	B3	Killinierin	21	F1
Halfway	23	F3	Kilbrittain	23	F3	Killinkere	11	E3
Halltown	11	E4	Kilcaimin	15	D3	Killinthomas	16	C3
Hamilton's Bawn	11	F1	Kilcar	4	B4	Killorglin	18	C4
Headford	15	D2	Kilcavan	16	B3	Killoscully	20	A1
Helen's Bay	7	E4	Kilchreest	15	E3	Killough, *Down*	13	D2
Herbertstown	19	F3	Kilcock	17	D2	Killough, *Wicklow*	17	E3

Name	Page	Grid	Name	Page	Grid	Name	Page	Grid
Killucan	16	C2	Kirkcubbin	13	D1	Lisbane	7	E4
Killukin	10	B3	Kishkeam	19	D4	Lisbellaw	11	D1
Killurin	21	E2	Knightstown	22	B2	Lisburn	7	D4
Killybegs	4	B4	Knock, *Clare*	19	D2	Liscannor	14	C4
Killyclogher	5	E4	Knock, *Mayo*	9	E3	Liscarney	9	D4
Killyconnan	11	D3	Knock, *Tipperary*	16	A4	Liscarroll	19	E4
Killygordon	5	D3	Knock Airport	9	E3	Liscolman	6	C2
Killylea	11	E1	Knockaderry	19	E3	Lisdoonvarna	14	C4
Kilmacanogue	17	E3	Knockalough	19	D2	Lisdowney	20	C1
Kilmacrenan	5	D2	Knockananna	17	D4	Lisduff	11	E3
Kilmacthomas	20	C3	Knockanarrigan	17	D4	Lisgall	11	F3
Kilmaganny	20	C2	Knockanevin	19	F4	Lisgarode	15	F4
Kilmaine	9	E4	Knockbrack	5	D3	Lisgoold	20	A4
Kilmaley	15	D4	Knockbrandon	21	E1	Lislea	6	C3
Kilmallock	19	F3	Knockbridge	11	F3	Lismakin	16	A4
Kilmanagh	20	C1	Knockbrit	20	B2	Lismore	20	B3
Kilmanahan	20	B2	Knockcroghery	10	B4	Lisnageer	11	D2
Kilmeague	16	C3	Knocklong	19	F3	Lisnagry	19	F2
Kilmeedy	19	E3	Knockmore	9	D3	Lisnakill	20	C3
Kilmeena	8	C3	Knockmoyle	15	E3	Lisnamuck	5	F3
Kilmichael	23	E2	Knocknaboul	19	D4	Lisnarrick	10	C1
Kilmihill	19	D2	Knocknacarry	7	D2	Lisnaskea	11	D2
Kilmona	23	F2	Knocknacree	16	C4	Lispatrick	23	F3
Kilmoon	11	F4	Knocknagashel	19	D3	Lispole	18	B4
Kilmore, *Clare*	19	F2	Knocknagree	19	D4	Lisrodden	6	C3
Kilmore, *Mayo*	9	E3	Knocknalina	8	C2	Lisronagh	20	B2
Kilmore, *Wexford*	21	E3	Knockraha	23	F2	Lisryan	11	D4
Kilmore Quay	21	E3	Knocks	23	E3	Lissan	5	F4
Kilmorna	19	D3	Knocktopher	20	C2	Lissatinning Bridge	22	B2
Kilmorony	16	C4				Lisselton	18	C3
Kilmurry	19	E2	**L**			Lissiniska	10	B1
Kilmurry McMahon	19	D2	Laban	15	D3	Lissycasey	19	D2
Kilmyshall	21	E1	Labasheeda	19	D2	Listerlin	21	D2
Kilnagross	10	B3	Lack	5	D4	Listooder	13	D1
Kilnaleck	11	D3	Lackamore	19	F2	Listowel	19	D3
Kilnamanagh	21	F2	Lackan	11	D4	Listry	18	C4
Kilnock	9	E4	Ladysbridge	20	A4	Littleton	20	B1
Kilquiggin	21	E1	Lagavara	6	C2	Lixnaw	18	C3
Kilrane	21	F3	Laghey	4	C4	Lobinstown	11	F3
Kilrea	6	C3	Laghtgeorge	15	D2	Loghill	19	D2
Kilrean	4	C3	Lahardaun	9	D2	Londonderry (Derry)	5	E3
Kilreekill	15	E3	Lahinch	14	C4	Longford	10	C4
Kilronan	14	B3	Lanesborough	10	B4	Longwood	16	C2
Kilross, *Donegal*	5	D3	Laracor	16	C2	Loskeran	20	B4
Kilross, *Tipperary*	20	A2	Laragh	17	E4	Lough Gowna	11	D3
Kilrush	19	D2	Largan	9	E2	Loughanure	4	C3
Kilsallagh	9	F4	Larne	7	E3	Loughbrickland	12	C1
Kilsaran	11	F3	Lauragh	22	C3	Lougher	18	B4
Kilshanchoe	16	C2	Laurencetown	15	F3	Loughgall	11	F1
Kilshanny	14	C4	Lavagh	9	F2	Loughglinn	9	F3
Kilskeer	11	E4	Lawrencetown	12	C1	Loughlinisland	13	D1
Kilskeery	10	C1	Leabgarrow	4	B3	Loughmoe	20	B1
Kiltartan	15	D3	Leamlara	20	A4	Loughrea	15	E3
Kiltealy	21	E1	Leap	23	E3	Louisburgh	8	C4
Kilteel	17	D3	Lecarrow	10	B4	Louth	11	F3
Kilteely	19	F3	Leckaun	10	B2	Lower Ballinderry	7	D4
Kiltimagh	9	E3	Leenane	8	C4	Lucan	17	D2
Kiltogan	17	D4	Leggs	10	B1	Lukeswell	20	C2
Kiltoom	15	F2	Leighlinbridge	21	D1	Lullymore	16	C3
Kiltormer	15	F3	Leitrim, *Down*	12	C1	Lurgan, *Armagh*	11	F1
Kiltullagh	15	E3	Leitrim, *Leitrim*	10	B3	Lurgan, *Roscommon*	9	F3
Kiltyclogher	10	B1	Leixlip	17	D2	Lusk	12	C4
Kilwaughter	7	D3	Lemybrien	20	C3	Lyracrumpane	19	D3
Kilworth	20	A3	Lenan	5	E2	Lyre	19	E4
Kilworth Camp	20	A3	Lerrig	18	C3	Lyrenaglogh	20	A3
Kincon	9	D2	Letterbarra	4	C4			
Kindrum	5	D2	Letterbreen	10	C1	**M**		
Kingarrow	4	C3	Lettercallow	14	B2	Maam	8	C4
Kingscourt	11	E3	Letterfinish	22	C2	Maam Cross	14	C2
Kingsland	9	F3	Letterfrack	8	C4	Maas	4	B3
Kinlough	10	B1	Letterkenny	5	D3	MacGregor's Corner	7	D3
Kinnadoohy	8	C4	Lettermacaward	4	C3	Macosquin	5	F2
Kinnegad	16	C2	Lettermullen	14	B3	Macroom	23	E2
Kinnitty	16	A3	Levally	15	E2	Maganey	16	C4
Kinsale	23	F3	Lifford	5	E3	Maghanlawaun	22	C2
Kinsalebeg	20	B4	Limavady	5	F2	Maghera, *Donegal*	4	B4
Kinvara	15	D3	Limerick (Luimneach)	19	F2	Maghera, *Londonderry*	6	C3
Kinvarra	14	C2	Lisacul	9	F3	Magherafelt	6	C4

Magheralin	12	C1	Moneydig	6	C3	**N**		
Magheramason	5	E3	Moneygall	15	F4	Naas (An Nás)	17	D3
Maghery, *Armagh*	11	F1	Moneyglass	6	C3	Nad	19	E4
Maghery, *Donegal*	4	B3	Moneylahan	9	F1	Narin	4	B3
Magilligan	5	F2	Moneymore	6	C4	Naul	12	C4
Maguiresbridge	11	D1	Moneyneany	5	F3	Navan (An Uaimh)	11	F4
Mahoonagh	19	E3	Moneyreagh	7	E4	Neale	9	D4
Mainham	17	D2	Monilea	11	D4	Nealstown	16	A4
Malahide	17	E2	Monivea	15	E2	Nenagh (An Aonach)	15	F4
Malin	5	E1	Montpelier	19	F2	New Birmingham	20	B1
Malin Beg	4	A4	Mooncoin	20	C3	New Buildings	5	E3
Malin More	4	A4	Moone	16	C4	New Ferry	6	C3
Mallow (Mala)	19	F4	Moorfields	7	D3	New Inn, *Cavan*	11	D3
Manorcunningham	5	D3	Morley's Bridge	23	D2	New Inn, *Galway*	15	E2
Manorhamilton	10	B1	Moss-side	6	C2	New Inn, *Laois*	16	B3
Manseltown	20	B1	Mossley	7	D4	New Kildimo	19	E2
Manulla	9	D3	Mothel	20	C3	New Ross	21	D2
Markethill	11	F1	Mount Bellew	15	E2	Newbawn	21	D2
Marshalstown	21	E1	Mount Hamilton	5	F3	Newbliss	11	D2
Martinstown, *Antrim*	7	D3	Mount Norris	11	F2	Newbridge, *Galway*	15	E2
Martinstown, *Limerick*	19	F3	Mount Nugent	11	D3	Newbridge, *Limerick*	19	E2
Massford	12	C1	Mount Talbot	15	F2	Newcastle, *Down*	13	D2
Masshill	9	E2	Mountallen	10	B2	Newcastle, *Dublin*	17	D2
Mastergeehy	22	B2	Mountbolus	16	A3	Newcastle, *Galway*	15	E2
Matehy	23	F2	Mountcharles	4	C4	Newcastle, *Tipperary*	20	B3
Matry	11	E4	Mountcollins	19	D3	Newcastle, *Wicklow*	17	E3
Mauricemills	14	C4	Mountfield	5	E4	Newcastle West	19	E3
Maynooth	17	D2	Mountjoy, *Tyrone*	6	C4	Newcestown	23	E3
Mayo	9	E4	Mountjoy, *Tyrone*	5	E4	Newgrange	11	F4
Mayobridge	12	C2	Mountmellick	16	B3	Newinn	20	B2
May's Corner	12	C1	Mountrath	16	B4	Newmarket, *Cork*	19	E4
Meelick	15	F3	Mountshannon	15	E4	Newmarket, *Kilkenny*	20	C2
Meelin	19	E4	Moville	5	F2	Newmarket-on-Fergus	19	E2
Meenaclady	4	C2	Moy	11	F1	Newport, *Mayo*	9	D3
Meenacross	4	B3	Moyard	8	B4	Newport, *Tipperary*	19	F2
Meenanarwa	4	C3	Moyarget	6	C2	Newport Trench	6	C4
Meenavean	4	B4	Moyasta	18	C2	Newry	11	F2
Meenglass	5	D4	Moycullen	14	C2	Newton Cashel	10	C4
Meentullynagarn	4	B4	Moydow	10	C4	Newtown, *Cork*	19	F4
Meigh	11	F2	Moygashel	11	E1	Newtown, *Kildare*	16	C2
Menlough	15	D2	Moylaw	9	D2	Newtown, *Laois*	16	C4
Middletown	11	E1	Moylett	11	E3	Newtown, *Meath*	11	F3
Midfield	9	E3	Moylough	15	E2	Newtown, *Roscommon*	15	F2
Midleton	20	A4	Moymore	15	D4	Newtown, *Tipperary*	16	A4
Mile House	21	E2	Moynalty	11	E3	Newtown, *Tipperary*	20	A2
Milebush	7	E4	Moyne, *Longford*	10	C3	Newtown, *Waterford*	20	C3
Milestone	20	A1	Moyne, *Roscommon*	9	F3	Newtown Crommelin	7	D3
Milford, *Cork*	19	E3	Moyne, *Wicklow*	17	D4	Newtown Forbes	10	C4
Milford, *Donegal*	5	D2	Moyrus	14	B2	Newtown Gore	10	C2
Millbrook	11	D4	Moys	5	F3	Newtown Sandes	19	D3
Millford	11	F1	Moyvalley	16	C2	Newtownabbey	7	D4
Millisle	7	E4	Moyvore	10	C4	Newtownards	7	E4
Millstreet, *Cork*	23	E2	Moyvoughly	16	A2	Newtownbutler	11	D2
Millstreet, *Waterford*	20	B3	Mucklon	16	C2	Newtowncunningham	5	E3
Milltown, *Cavan*	11	D2	Muckross	23	D2	Newtownhamilton	11	F2
Milltown, *Down*	12	C2	Muff	5	E2	Newtownlow	16	B2
Milltown, *Galway*	9	E4	Muine Bheag	21	D1	Newtownlynch	15	D3
Milltown, *Kerry*	18	C4	Mullagh, *Cavan*	11	E3	Newtownmountkennedy	17	E3
Milltown, *Kerry*	18	A4	Mullagh, *Clare*	19	D1	Newtownstewart	5	E4
Milltown, *Kildare*	16	C3	Mullagh, *Mayo*	8	C4	Ninemilehouse	20	C2
Milltown, *Tyrone*	5	F4	Mullagh, *Meath*	17	D2	Nobber	11	E3
Milltown Malbay	14	C4	Mullaghmore	9	F1	Nohoval	23	F3
Minane Bridge	23	F3	Mullaghroe	9	F3	North Ring	23	E3
Mine Head	20	B4	Mullan, *Fermanagh*	10	C2	Noughaval	14	C4
Minerstown	13	D1	Mullan, *Monaghan*	11	E1	Nurney, *Carlow*	21	D1
Mitchelstown	20	A3	Mullany's Cross	9	E2	Nurney, *Kildare*	16	C3
Moate	16	A2	Mullartown	13	D2	Nutt's Corner	7	D4
Modreeny	15	F4	Mullinahone	20	C2			
Mogeely	20	A4	Mullinavat	20	C2	**O**		
Mohil	20	C1	Mullingar	16	B2	O'Briensbridge	19	F2
Mohill	10	C3	(Án Muileann gCearr)			Ogonelloe	15	E4
Moira	12	C1	Mulrany	8	C3	Oilgate	21	E2
Monaghan	11	E2	Multyfarnham	11	D4	Old Head	23	F3
(Muineachán)			Mungret	19	F2	Old Leighlin	21	D1
Monamolin	21	F1	Murley	11	D1	Old Ross	21	D2
Monasterevan	16	C3	Murntown	21	E3	Old Town, *Donegal*	5	D3
Monea	10	C1	Murroogh	14	C3	Old Town, *Roscommon*	16	A2
Moneen	15	D2	Myshall	21	D1	Oldcastle	11	D4

Name	Page	Grid
Oldcourt	17	D3
Oldtown	17	D2
Omagh	5	E4
Omeath	12	C2
Onaght	14	B3
Oola	20	A2
Oran	10	B4
Oranmore	15	D3
Oristown	11	E4
Oughterard	14	C2
Oulart	21	E2
Ovens	23	F2
Owenbeg	9	E2
Oysterhaven	23	F3

P

Name	Page	Grid
Pallas Green	19	F2
Pallaskenry	19	E2
Palmerston	17	D2
Park	5	F3
Parkmore	15	D3
Parknasilla	22	C2
Partry	9	D4
Passage East	21	D3
Passage West	23	F2
Patrickswell	19	F2
Peterswell	15	D3
Pettigo	5	D4
Pharis	6	C2
Pipers Town	10	C3
Pluck	5	D3
Plumbridge	5	E4
Pollatomish	8	C1
Pomeroy	5	F4
Pontoon	9	D3
Port, *Donegal*	4	B4
Port, *Louth*	12	C3
Portacloy	8	C1
Portadown	11	F1
Portaferry	13	D1
Portaleen	5	E1
Portarlington	16	B3
Portavogie	13	E1
Portballintrae	6	C2
Portglenone	6	C3
Portland	15	F3
Portlaoise	16	B4
Portlaw	20	C3
Portmagee	22	A2
Portmarnock	17	E2
Portmuck	7	E3
Portnoo	4	B3
Portrane	17	E2
Portroe	15	E4
Portrush	6	C2
Portsalon	5	D2
Portstewart	5	F2
Portumna	15	F3
Porturlin	8	C1
Poulgorm Bridge	23	D2
Poulnamucky	20	B2
Power's Cross	15	F3
Poyntz Pass	11	F1
Priesthaggard	21	D2
Prosperous	16	C2
Puckaun	15	F4

Q

Name	Page	Grid
Querrin	18	C2
Quin	15	D4

R

Name	Page	Grid
Raffrey	13	D1
Raghly	9	F1
Rahan	16	A3
Raheen	23	F2
Ramelton	5	D2
Randalstown	6	C4
Rapemills	16	A3
Raphoe	5	D3
Rasharkin	6	C3
Rashedoge	5	D3
Rath	16	A3
Rathangan	16	C3
Rathcabban	15	F3
Rathconrath	16	B2
Rathcool	19	E4
Rathcoole	17	D3
Rathcor	12	C3
Rathcormac	20	A3
Rathdangan	17	D4
Rathdowney	16	A4
Rathdrum	17	E4
Rathfarnham	17	E2
Rathfriland	12	C2
Rathgormuck	20	C2
Rathkeale	19	E3
Rathkeevin	20	B2
Rathkenny	11	F4
Rathlackan	9	D1
Rathlee	9	E1
Rathluirc (Charleville)	19	F3
Rathmolyon	16	C2
Rathmore, *Kerry*	19	D4
Rathmore, *Kildare*	17	D3
Rathmullan	5	D2
Rathnew	17	E4
Rathnure	21	D2
Rathowen	11	D4
Rathumney	21	D3
Rathvilly	17	D4
Ratoath	17	D2
Ravensdale	11	F2
Reaghstown	11	F3
Reanaclogheen	20	B4
Reanagowan	18	C3
Reananeree	23	E2
Reanascreena	23	E3
Rear Cross	20	A1
Recess	14	B2
Redcastle	5	E2
Redcross	17	E4
Redhills	11	D2
Reen	22	C2
Reens	19	E3
Rerrin	22	C3
Rhode	16	B2
Richhill	11	F1
Ringaskiddy	20	A4
Ringsend	5	F2
Ringville	20	B4
Rinneen	14	C4
Rinvyle	8	B4
Riverchapel	21	F1
Riverstown, *Cork*	23	F2
Riverstown, *Sligo*	9	F2
Riverstown, *Tipperary*	16	A3
Roadford	14	C4
Robertstown	16	C3
Rochestown	21	D2
Rochfortbridge	16	B2
Rockcorry	11	E2
Rockhill	19	F3
Rockmills	19	F4
Rooaun	15	F3
Rookchapel	19	D4
Roonah Quay	8	C4
Roosky, *Mayo*	9	F3
Roosky, *Roscommon*	10	C3
Rosapenna	5	D2
Rosbeg	4	B3
Rosbercon	21	D2
Roscommon	10	B4
Roscrea	16	A4
Rosegreen	20	B2
Rosenallis	16	B3
Rosmuck	14	B2
Ross	11	D3
Ross Carbery	23	E3
Rossaveel	14	C2
Rossbrin	23	D4
Rosscahill	14	C2
Rosscor	10	B1
Rosses Point	9	F1
Rossinver	10	B1
Rosslare	21	F3
Rosslare Harbour	21	F3
Rosslea	11	D2
Rossnowlagh	4	C4
Rostellan	20	A4
Rostrevor	12	C2
Rosturk	8	C3
Roundfort	9	E4
Roundstone	14	B2
Roundwood	17	E3
Rousky	5	E4
Ruan	15	D4
Rubane	13	D1
Rush	17	E2
Ryefield	11	E3
Rylane Cross	23	E2

S

Name	Page	Grid
Saggart	17	D3
Saint Johnstown	5	E3
Saintfield	13	D1
Saliahig	22	B2
Sallins	17	D3
Sallypark	15	F4
Salruck	8	C4
Salthill	15	D3
Saul	13	D1
Scalva	11	F1
Scardaun	10	B4
Scarriff	15	E4
Scartaglen	19	D4
Schull	23	D4
Scotch Corner	11	E2
Scotch Town	5	E4
Scotshouse	11	D2
Scotstown	11	E2
Scramoge	10	B4
Screeb	14	C2
Screen	21	E2
Screggan	16	A3
Scribbagh	10	B1
Seapatrick	12	C1
Seskinore	11	D1
Shalwy	4	B4
Shanacashel	22	C2
Shanacrane	23	E3
Shanagarry	20	A4
Shanagolden	19	E2
Shanavogh	14	C4
Shankill	17	E3
Shannon Airport	19	E2
Shannonbridge	15	F3
Shantonagh	11	E2
Shanvus	10	B1
Sharavogue	16	A4
Shercock	11	E3
Sheskin	8	C2
Shillelagh	21	E1
Shinrone	16	A4
Shoptown	7	D3
Shrigley	13	D1
Shrule	15	D2
Silvermines	20	A1
Sion Mills	5	E3
Six Crosses	19	D3
Six Road Ends	7	E4
Sixmilebridge	19	E2
Sixmilecross	5	F4
Skerries	12	C4

Name	Page	Grid
Skibbereen	23	D4
Slane	11	F4
Sligo (Sligeach)	9	F1
Smerwick	18	A4
Smithborough	11	E2
Smithstown	20	C1
Snave Bridge	23	D3
Sneem	22	C2
Spa	18	C4
Spanish Point	14	C4
Spiddal	14	C3
Spink	16	B4
Springfield	10	C1
Srah	9	D4
Srahmore	9	D3
Srahnamanragh Bridge	8	C2
Sranea	10	B1
Staffordstown	6	C4
Stamullen	12	C4
Stepaside	17	E3
Stewartstown	6	C4
Stillorgan	17	E2
Stonefield	8	C1
Stoneyford	20	C2
Stonyford	7	D4
Strabane	5	E3
Stradbally, *Kerry*	18	B4
Stradbally, *Laois*	16	C4
Stradbally, *Waterford*	20	C3
Stradone	11	D3
Straffan	17	D2
Strand	19	E3
Strandhill	9	F2
Strangford	13	D1
Stranocum	6	C2
Stranorlar	5	D3
Stratford	17	D4
Streamstown	16	A2
Strokestown	10	B4
Summerhill	17	D2
Suncroft	16	C3
Swan	16	C4
Swanlinbar	10	C2
Swan's Cross Roads	11	E2
Swatragh	6	C3
Swinford	9	E3
Swords	17	E3

T

Name	Page	Grid
Taghmon	21	E2
Tahilla	22	C2
Tallaght	17	D2
Tallanstown	11	F3
Tallow	20	A3
Tamlaght	6	C3
Tamney	5	D2
Tandragee	11	F1
Tang	16	A2
Tangaveane	4	C3
Tarbert	19	D2
Tassagh	11	F2
Taur	19	D4
Tawnyinah	9	F3
Taylor's Cross	15	F3
Teelin	4	B4
Teemore	11	D2
Teeranearagh	22	B2
Teerelton	23	E2
Teevurcher	11	E3
Templeboy	9	E2
Templederry	20	A1
Templeglentan	19	D3
Templemore	20	B1
Templenoe	22	C2
Templepatrick	7	D4
Templetown	21	D3
Templetuohy	20	B1
Tempo	11	D1

Name	Page	Grid
Terenure	17	E2
Termon	5	D2
Termonfeckin	12	C4
Terrin	11	D4
Terryglass	15	F3
The Diamond, *Tyrone*	5	E4
The Diamond, *Tyrone*	6	C4
The Harrow	21	E1
The Loup	6	C4
The Pike	20	A4
The Rock	5	F4
The Sheddings	7	D3
The Six Towns	5	F3
The Temple	12	C1
Thomastown	21	D2
Thurles (Durlas)	20	B1
Tiduff	18	A4
Tildarg	7	D3
Timahoe, *Kildare*	16	C2
Timahoe, *Laois*	16	B4
Timoleague	23	F3
Timolin	16	C4
Tinahely	17	D4
Tipperary	20	A2
Toames	23	E2
Tober	16	A2
Tobermore	6	C3
Toberscanavan	9	F2
Togher, *Cork*	23	E3
Togher, *Louth*	12	C3
Togher, *Offaly*	16	A2
Tomdarragh	17	E3
Toomard	15	E2
Toombeola	14	B2
Toomebridge	6	C4
Toomyvara	15	F4
Tooraree	19	D3
Toormore	22	C4
Torr	7	D2
Tourmakeady	9	D4
Tower	23	F2
Trafrask	22	C3
Tralee (Trá Lí)	18	C4
Tramore (Trá Mhór)	21	D3
Trean	9	D4
Treantagh	5	D3
Treehoo	11	D2
Trillick	11	D1
Trim	11	E4
Trory	10	C1
Trust	15	E2
Tuam	15	D2
Tuamgraney	15	E4
Tubber	15	D4
Tubbercurry	9	F2
Tubbrid	20	C1
Tulla	15	D4
Tullaghan	10	B1
Tullamore (Tulach Mhór)	16	B3
Tullaroan	20	C1
Tullogher	21	D2
Tullow	21	E1
Tully, *Donegal*	4	C4
Tully, *Fermanagh*	11	D2
Tully, *Fermanagh*	10	C1
Tully Cross	8	B4
Tullyallen	11	F4
Tullycanna	21	E3
Tullyhogue	5	F4
Tullyvin	11	D2
Tullyvoos	4	C4
Tulsk	10	B4
Turlough, *Clare*	15	D3
Turlough, *Mayo*	9	D3
Turreen	10	B4
Two Mile Bridge	16	B3
Twomileborris	20	B1

Name	Page	Grid
Tydavnet	11	E1
Tyholland	11	E2
Tylas	11	F4
Tynan	11	E1
Tyrella	13	D2
Tyrrellspass	16	B2

U

Name	Page	Grid
Unionhall	23	E4
Upperchurch	20	A1
Upperlands	6	C3
Urlingford	20	B1

V

Name	Page	Grid
Valley	8	C2
Valleymount	17	D3
Ventry	18	A4
Vicarstown	16	C3
Villierstown	20	B3
Virginia	11	E3
Vow	6	C3

W

Name	Page	Grid
Waddingtown	21	E3
Walterstown	11	F4
Waringsford	12	C1
Waringstown	12	C1
Warrenpoint	12	C2
Waterfall	23	F2
Waterford (Port Láirgé)	21	D3
Watergrasshill	20	A4
Waterside	5	E4
Waterville	22	B2
Wattlebridge	11	D2
Wellington Bridge	21	E3
West Town	4	C1
Westport	9	D3
Westport Quay	9	D3
Wexford (Loch Garman)	21	E2
Wheathill	10	C2
White Hall	23	D4
Whitechurch, *Cork*	23	F2
Whitechurch, *Waterford*	20	B3
Whitecross	11	F2
Whitegate, *Clare*	15	E4
Whitegate, *Cork*	20	A4
Whitehall, *Kilkenny*	21	D1
Whitehall, *Roscommon*	10	C4
Whitehead	7	E3
Whitehouse	7	D4
Wicklow (Cill Mhantáin)	17	E4
Wilkinstown	11	F4
Willbrook	15	D4
Windgap	20	C2
Windmill	16	C2
Wolfhill	16	C4
Woodenbridge	17	E4
Woodford	15	E3
Woodstown	21	D3
Woodtown	11	F3

Y

Name	Page	Grid
Youghal (Eochaill)	20	B4